D1070217

Mumbai
& Gujarat

David Stott & Victoria McCulloch

Credits

Footprint credits
Editor: Nicola Gibbs
Production and layout: Emma Bryers
Maps: Kevin Feeney

Managing Director: Andy Riddle
Commercial Director: Patrick Dawson
Publisher: Alan Murphy
Publishing Managers: Felicity Laughton,
Nicola Gibbs
Digital Editors: Jo Williams, Tom Mellors
Marketing and PR: Liz Harper
Sales: Diane McEntee
Advertising: Renu Sibal
Finance and Administration:
Elizabeth Taylor

Photography credits
Front cover: BasPhoto / Shutterstock
Back cover: Paul Prescott / Shutterstock

Printed and bound in the United States
of America

Every effort has been made to ensure that
the facts in this guidebook are accurate.
However, travellers should still obtain
advice from consulates, airlines, etc,
about travel and visa requirements before
travelling. The authors and publishers
cannot accept responsibility for any loss,
injury or inconvenience however caused.

Publishing information
Footprint *Focus Mumbai & Gujarat*
1st edition
© Footprint Handbooks Ltd
October 2011

ISBN: 978 1 908206 41 1
CIP DATA: A catalogue record for this book
is available from the British Library

® Footprint Handbooks and the
Footprint mark are a registered
trademark of Footprint Handbooks Ltd

Published by Footprint
6 Riverside Court
Lower Bristol Road
Bath BA2 3DZ, UK
T +44 (0)1225 469141
F +44 (0)1225 469461
www.footprinttravelguides.com

Distributed in the USA by Globe Pequot Press,
Guilford, Connecticut

The content of Footprint *Focus Mumbai &
Gujarat* has been taken directly from
Footprint's *India Handbook*, which was
researched and written by David Stott,
Vanessa Betts and Victoria McCulloch.

Contents

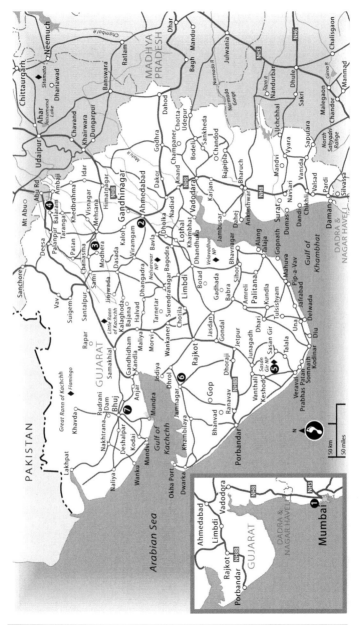

Maximum City, the City of Dreams, India's economic capital and melting pot; you can throw epithets and superlatives at Mumbai until the cows come home, but it refuses to be understood on a merely intellectual level. Like London and New York, it's a restless human tapestry of cultures, religions, races, ways of surviving and thriving, and one that evokes palpable emotion; whether you love it or hate it, you can't stay unaffected.

Unsurprisingly, India's largest city is served by the country's busiest airport, with a staggering 25 million passengers each year. A major transport hub and gateway for exploring the rest of the country, it is just a hop, skip and a train ride away from the neighbouring state of Gujarat. Once incorporated into the state of Bombay, the Gujarati-speaking region gained independence in 1960 but retains many cultural and ethnic ties.

From the stunning salt plains of the Great Rann of Kachcch in the north to the jungle of Sasan Gir National Park in the south, Gujarat is a fascinating state with picturesque landscapes and some of the world's oldest ports. It has the fastest-growing economy and is one of the most industrial states – mills and factories dot the horizon. Yet for all its rewards, it remains squarely off the radar of mainstream tourism, and makes a challenging place for independent travel.

Planning your trip

When to go

Mumbai is hot during the daytime throughout the year, it is also very humid. Average daily temperatures are 28°C in January and 33°C in May, although night-time temperatures fall considerably from November to March. The southwest monsoon normally breaks on the coast in the second week of June and finishes in September, bringing most of the region's rain in often prolonged and violent storms.

In Ahmedabad the maximum winter temperature is 27°C, although nights are cold and sub-zero cold spells have been recorded. In summer it is extremely hot and maximum temperatures can reach 48°C. Further south the winter temperatures never fall as far, and the summer temperatures are slightly more moderate. In the far south, around Daman, rainfall is still strongly affected by the southwest monsoon and often exceeds 1500 mm, nearly all between June and October. However, because Gujarat is marginal to the main rain-bearing winds the total amounts are highly variable, decreasing rapidly northwards. Ahmedabad normally receives about 900 mm a year while Kachchh, on the borders of the true desert, has recorded less than 25 mm.

Getting there

Air

India is accessible by air from virtually every continent. Most international flights arrive in Delhi, Mumbai, Chennai or Kolkata. There are also international airports in several other cities (eg Ahmedabad, Bengaluru (Bangalore), Hyderabad, Thiruvananthapuram, Goa), some of which allow customs formalities to be completed there although the flight may be routed through a principal airport. Some carriers permit 'open-jaw' travel, arriving in, and departing from, different cities in India. Some (eg **Air India, British Airways**) have convenient non-stop flights from Europe, eg from London to Delhi, takes only nine hours.

Alternatively, you can fly to numerous destinations across India with **Jet Airways** or **Kingfisher**. The prices are very competitive if domestic flights are booked in conjunction with Jet on the international legs. In 2011 the cheapest return flights to Delhi from London started from around £400, but leapt to £800+ as you approached the high season of Christmas, New Year and Easter.

From Europe Despite the increases to Air Passenger Duty, Britain remains the cheapest place in Europe for flights to India. **Virgin Atlantic, British Airways** and **Kingfisher** fly from London to Delhi in 8½ hours or Mumbai in 9½ hours. From mainland Europe, **Jet Airways** flies to India from Brussels and Milan, while major European flag carriers including **KLM** and **Lufthansa** fly to Delhi and/or Mumbai from their respective hub airports. In most cases the cheapest flights are with Middle Eastern or Central Asian airlines, transiting via airports in the Gulf. Several airlines from the Middle East (eg **Emirates, Gulf Air, Kuwait Airways, Royal Jordanian, Qatar Airways, Oman Air**) offer good discounts to Mumbai and other Indian regional capitals from London, but fly via their hub cities, adding to the journey time. Consolidators in the UK can quote some competitive fares, such as: **Flightbookers**, T0871-

Don't miss ...

223 5000, www.ebookers.com; North South Travel, T01245-608291, www.northsouth travel.co.uk (profits to charity).

From North America From the east coast, several airlines including **Air India**, **Jet Airways**, **Continental** and **Delta** fly direct from New York to Delhi and Mumbai. **American** flies to both cities from Chicago. Discounted tickets on **British Airways**, **KLM**, **Lufthansa**, **Gulf Air** and **Kuwait Airways** are sold through agents although they will invariably fly via their country's capital cities. From the west coast, **Air India** flies from Los Angeles to Delhi and Mumbai, and **Jet Airways** from San Francisco to Mumbai via Shanghai. Alternatively, fly via Hong Kong, Singapore or Bangkok using one of those countries' national carriers. **Air Canada** operates between Vancouver and Delhi. **Air Brokers International**, www.airbrokers.com, is competitive and reputable. **STA**, www.statravel.co.uk, has offices in many US cities, Toronto and Ontario. Student fares are also available from **Travel Cuts**, www.travelcuts.com, in Canada.

From Australasia Qantas, Singapore Airlines, Thai Airways, Malaysian Airlines, Cathay Pacific and Air India are the principal airlines connecting the continents, although Qantas is the only one that flies direct, with services from Sydney to Mumbai. **Tiger Airways** run a no-frills service from Darwin to Kochi via Singapore, and **Air Asia X** operates from Melbourne and the Gold Coast to several South Indian cities via Kuala Lumpur; these flights can be much cheaper than standard airlines, at the cost of extended layovers and the usual extra charges for checked luggage, food etc. STA and **Flight Centre** offer discounted tickets from their branches in major cities in Australia and New Zealand. **Abercrombie & Kent**, www.abercrombiekent.co.uk, **Adventure World**, www.adventureworld.net.au, **Peregrine**, www.peregrineadventures.com, and **Travel Corporation of India**, www.tcindia.com, organize tours.

Airport information The formalities on arrival in India have been increasingly streamlined during the last few years and the facilities at the major international airports greatly improved. However, arrival can still be a slow process. Disembarkation cards, with an attached customs declaration, are handed out to passengers during the inward flight. The immigration form should be handed in at the immigration counter on arrival. The customs slip will be returned, for handing over to the customs on leaving the baggage collection hall.

You may well find that there are delays of over an hour at immigration in processing passengers passing through immigration who need help with filling in forms.

Departure tax Rs 500 is payable for all international departures other than those to neighbouring SAARC countries, when the tax is Rs 250 (not reciprocated by Sri Lanka). This is normally included in your international ticket; check when buying. (To save time 'Security Check' your baggage before checking in at departure.)

Getting around

Air
India has a comprehensive network linking the major cities of the different states. Deregulation of the airline industry has had a transformative effect on travel within India, with a host of low-budget private carriers offering sometimes unbelievably cheap fares on an ever-expanding network of routes in a bid to woo the train-travelling middle class. Promotional fares as low as Rs 9 (US$0.20) are not unknown, though such numbers are rendered somewhat meaningless by additional taxes and fuel charges – an extra US$30-50 on most flights. On any given day, booking a few days in advance, you can expect to fly between Delhi and Mumbai for around US$100 one way including taxes, while a month's notice and flying with a no-frills airline can reduce the price to US$70-80; regional routes, eg Mumbai–Kozhikode in north Kerala, are often cheaper than routes between main cities.

Competition from the efficiently run private sector has, in general, improved the quality of services provided by the nationalized airlines. It also seems to herald the end of the two-tier pricing structure, meaning that ticket prices are now usually the same for foreign and Indian travellers. The airport authorities too have made efforts to improve handling on the ground.

Although flying is comparatively expensive, for covering vast distances or awkward links on a route it is an option worth considering, though delays and re-routing can be irritating. For short distances, and on some routes (eg Delhi–Agra–Delhi), it makes more sense to travel by train. If you don't want to take a connecting flight down to Goa, the Konkan railway makes a pretty, and increasingly speedy, alternative. Don't be tempted to take the bus.

The best way to get an idea of the current routes, carriers and fares is to use a third-party booking website such as www.cheapairticketsindia.com (toll-free numbers: UK T0800-101 0928, USA T1-888 825 8680), www.cleartrip.com, www.makemytrip.co.in, or www.yatra.com. Booking with these is a different matter: some refuse foreign credit cards outright, while others have to be persuaded to give your card special clearance. Tickets booked on these sites are typically issued as an email ticket or an SMS text message – the simplest option if you have an Indian mobile phone, though it must be converted to a paper ticket at the relevant carrier's airport offices before you will be allowed into the terminal. Makemytrip.com and Travelocity.com both accept international credit cards.

Rail
Trains can still be the cheapest and most comfortable means of travelling long distances saving you hotel expenses on overnight journeys. It gives access to booking station Retiring Rooms, which can be useful from time to time. Above all, you have an ideal opportunity to meet local travellers and catch a glimpse of life on the ground. Remember the dark glass on air-conditioned coaches does restrict vision. See also www.indianrail.gov.in.

Train touts

Many railway stations – and some bus stations and major tourist sites – are heavily populated with touts. Self-styled 'agents' will board trains before they enter the station and seek out tourists, often picking up their luggage and setting off with words such as "Madam!/Sir! Come with me madam/sir! You need top-class hotel …". They will even select porters to take your luggage without giving you any say.

If you have succeeded in getting off the train or even in obtaining a trolley you will find hands eager to push it for you.

For a first-time visitor such touts can be more than a nuisance. You need to keep calm and firm. Decide in advance where you want to stay. If you need a porter on trains, select one yourself and agree a price **before** the porter sets off with your baggage. If travelling with a companion one can stay guarding the luggage while the other gets hold of a taxi and negotiates the price to the hotel. It sounds complicated and sometimes it feels it. The most important thing is to behave as if you know what you are doing!

High-speed trains There are several air-conditioned 'high-speed' **Shatabdi** (or 'Century') **Express** for day travel, and **Rajdhani Express** ('Capital City') for overnight journeys. These cover large sections of the network but due to high demand you need to book them well in advance (up to 90 days). Meals and drinks are usually included.

Royal trains You can travel like a maharaja on the **Palace on Wheels** (www.palaceon wheels.net), the famous seven-nighter which has been running for many years and gives visitors an opportunity to see some of the 'royal' cities in Rajasthan during the winter months for around US$2500. A wonderful way to travel but time at the destinations is a little compressed for some. Two other seven-nighters are the **Deccan Odyssey** (www.indiarail.co.uk/do.htm), a train running in Maharashtra, and the **Golden Chariot** (www.indiarail.co.uk/gt.htm), a relatively new option running in Karnataka covering Belur, Halebid, Shravanabelagola and then Hampi and Badami/Aihole/Pattadakal. The **Heritage on Wheels** (www.heritageonwheels.org.in), a meter-gauge train covering the Shekawati region, Tal Chappar and Bikaner, starts and concludes in Jaipur. Bookings and more information for all these heritage-style trains is available at www.indrail.co.uk.

Steam For rail enthusiasts, the steam-hauled narrow-gauge trains between Kurseong and Darjeeling in North Bengal (a World Heritage Site), and between Mettupalayam and Coonoor, and a special one between Ooty and Runnymede in the Nilgiris, are an attraction. See the IRCTC and Indian Railways website, www.irctc.co.in. **Williams Travel**, 18/20 Howard St, Belfast BT1 6FQ, Northern Ireland, T028-9023 0714, www.williams-travel.co.uk, and SDEL (see page 10) are recommended for tailor-made trips.

Classes A/c First Class, available only on main routes, is very comfortable (bedding provided). It will also be possible for tourists to reserve special coaches (some air conditioning) which are normally allocated to senior railway officials only. **A/c Sleeper**, two and three-tier configurations (known as 2AC and 3AC), are clean and comfortable and popular with middle class families; these are the safest carriages for women travelling alone. **A/c Executive Class**, with wide reclining seats, are available on many Shatabdi trains at double the price of the ordinary **a/c Chair Car** which are equally comfortable. **First Class (non-a/c)** is gradually being phased out, and is now restricted to a handful of routes in the south, but the run-down old carriages still provide a pleasant experience if you like open windows. **Second Class (non-a/c)** two and three-tier (commonly called **Sleeper**), provides exceptionally cheap and atmospheric travel, with basic padded vinyl seats and open windows that allow the sights and sounds of India (not to mention dust, insects and flecks of spittle expelled by passengers up front) to drift into the carriage. On long journeys Sleeper can be crowded and uncomfortable, and toilet facilities can be unpleasant; it is nearly always better to use the Indian-style squat loos rather than the Western-style ones as they are better maintained. At the bottom rung is **Unreserved Second Class**, with hard wooden benches. You can travel long distances for a trivial amount of money, but unreserved carriages are often ridiculously crowded, and getting off at your station may involve a battle of will and strength against the hordes trying to shove their way on.

Indrail passes These allow travel across the network without having to pay extra reservation fees and sleeper charges but you have to spend a high proportion of your time on the train to make it worthwhile. However, the advantages of pre-arranged reservations and automatic access to 'Tourist Quotas' can tip the balance in favour of the pass for some travellers.

Tourists (foreigners and Indians resident abroad) may buy these passes from the tourist sections of principal railway booking offices and pay in foreign currency, major credit cards, travellers' cheques or rupees with encashment certificates. Fares range from US$57 to US$1060 for adults or half that for children. Rail-cum-air tickets are also to be made available.

Indrail passes can also conveniently be bought abroad from special agents. For people contemplating a single long journey soon after arriving in India, the Half- or One-day Pass with a confirmed reservation is worth the peace of mind; two- or four-day passes are also sold.

The UK agent is **SDEL**, 103 Wembley Park Drive, Wembley, Middlesex HA9 8HG, UK, T020-8903 3411, www.indiarail.co.uk. They make all necessary reservations and offer excellent advice. They can also book Indian Airlines and Jet Airways internal flights.

A **White Pass** allows first class a/c travel (the top rung); a **Green**, a/c two-tier Sleepers and Chair Cars; and the **Yellow**, only second-class travel. Passes for up to four days' duration are only sold abroad.

Cost A/c first class costs about double the rate for two-tier shown below, and non a/c second class about half. Children (aged five to 12) travel at half the adult fare. The young (12-30 years) and senior citizens (65 years and over) are allowed a 30% discount on journeys over 500 km (just show your passport).

Period	US$ A/c 2-tier	Period	US$ A/c 2-tier
½ day	26	21 days	198
1 day	43	30 days	248
7 days	135	60 days	400
15 days	185	90 days	530

Fares for individual journeys are based on distance covered and reflect both the class and the type of train. Higher rates apply on the Mail and Express trains and the air-conditioned Shatabdi and Rajdhani Expresses.

Internet services Much information is available online via www.railtourismindia.com, www.indianrail.gov.in and www.trainenquiry.com, where you can check timetables (which change frequently), numbers, seat availability and even the running status of your train. Internet e-tickets can be bought and printed on www.irctc.in – a great time-saver when the system works properly. The credit card process can be complicated, and at time of writing is off-limits to credit cards issued outside India. The best option is to use a third-party agent such as www.makemytrip.com or www.cleartrip.com, which provide an easily understood booking engine and accept foreign cards. An alternative is to seek a local agent who can sell e-tickets, which can cost as little as Rs 5-10 (plus Rs 20 reservation fee, some agents charge up to Rs 150 a ticket, however), and can save hours of hassle; simply present the printout to the ticket collector. However, it is tricky if you then want to cancel an e-ticket which an agent has bought for you on their account.

Note All train numbers changed to five-digit numbers in 2010-2011; in most cases, adding a '1' to the start of an old four-figure number will produce the new number. Otherwise, try your luck with the 'train number enquiry' search at www.indianrail.gov.in/inet_trnno_enq.html.

Tickets and reservations It is now possible to reserve tickets for virtually any train on the network from one of the 1000 computerized reservation centres across India. It is always best to book as far in advance as possible (usually up to 60 days). To reserve a seat on a particular train, note down the train's name, number and departure time and fill in a reservation form while you line up at the ticket window; you can use one form for up to four passengers. At busy stations the wait can take an hour or more. You can save a lot of time and effort by asking a travel agent to get your tickets for a fee of Rs 50-100. If the class you want is full, ask if special 'quotas' are available (see above). If not, consider buying a 'wait list' ticket, as seats often become available close to the train's departure time; phone the station on the day of departure to check your ticket's status. If you don't have a reservation for a particular train but carry an Indrail Pass, you may get one by arriving three hours early. Be wary of touts at the station offering tickets, hotels or exchange.

Timetables Regional timetables are available cheaply from station bookstalls; the monthly *Indian Bradshaw* is sold in principal stations. The handy *Trains at a Glance* (Rs 30) lists popular trains likely to be used by most foreign travellers and is available at stalls at Indian railway stations and in the UK from SDEL (see page 10).

Road

Road travel is often the only choice for reaching many of the places of outstanding interest in which India is so rich. For the uninitiated, travel by road can also be a worrying experience because of the apparent absence of conventional traffic regulations and also in the mountains, especially during the rainy season when landslides are possible. Vehicles drive on the left – in theory. Routes around the major cities are usually crowded with lorry traffic, especially at night, and the main roads are often poor and slow. There are a few motorway-style expressways, but most main roads are single track. Some district roads are quiet, and although they are not fast they can be a good way of seeing the country and village life if you have the time.

Bus Buses now reach virtually every part of India, offering a cheap, if often uncomfortable, means of visiting places off the rail network. Very few villages are now more than 2-3 km from a bus stop. Services are run by the State Corporation from the State Bus Stand (and private companies which often have offices nearby). The latter allow advance reservations, including booking printable e-tickets online (check www.redbus.in and www.viaworld.in) and, although tickets prices are a little higher, they have fewer stops and are a bit more comfortable. In the absence of trains, buses are often the only budget option, into the Himalaya for example. There are many sleeper buses (a contradiction in terms) running Mumbai–Goa or into the Himalaya – if you must take a sleeper bus, choose a lower berth near the front of the bus. The upper berths are almost always really uncomfortable.

Bus categories Though comfortable for sightseeing trips, apart from the very best 'sleeper coaches' even **air-conditioned luxury coaches** can be very uncomfortable for really long journeys. Often the air conditioning is very cold so wrap up. Journeys over 10 hours can be extremely tiring so it is better to go by train if there is a choice. **Express buses** run over long distances (frequently overnight), these are often called 'video coaches' and can be an appalling experience unless you appreciate loud film music blasting through the night. Ear plugs and eye masks may ease the pain. They rarely average more than 45 kph. **Local buses** are often very crowded, quite bumpy, slow and usually poorly maintained. However, over short distances, they can be a very cheap, friendly and easy way of getting about. Even where signboards are not in English someone will usually give you directions. Many larger towns have **minibus** services which charge a little more than the buses and pick up and drop passengers on request. Again very crowded, and with restricted headroom, they are the fastest way of getting about many of the larger towns.

Bus travel tips Some towns have different bus stations for different destinations. Booking on major long-distance routes is now computerized. Book in advance where possible and avoid the back of the bus where it can be very bumpy. If your destination is only served by a local bus you may do better to take the Express bus and 'persuade' the driver, with a tip in advance, to stop where you want to get off. You will have to pay the full fare to the first stop beyond your destination but you will get there faster and more comfortably. When an unreserved bus pulls into a bus station, there is usually an unholy scramble for seats, whilst those arriving have to struggle to get off! In many areas there is an unwritten 'rule of reservation' using handkerchiefs or bags thrust through the windows to reserve seats. Some visitors may feel a more justified right to a seat having fought their way through the crowd, but it is generally best to do as local people do and be prepared with a handkerchief or 'sarong'. As soon as it touches the seat, it is yours! Leave it on your seat when getting off to use the toilet at bus stations.

Car A car provides a chance to travel off the beaten track, and gives unrivalled opportunities for seeing something of India's great variety of villages and small towns. Until recently, the most widely used hire car was the Hindustan Ambassador. However, except for the newest model, they are often very unreliable, and although they still have their devotees, many find them uncomfortable for long journeys. For a similar price, Maruti cars and vans (Omni) are much more reliable and are now the preferred choice in many areas. Gypsy 4WDs and Jeeps are also available, especially in the hills, where larger Sumos have made an appearance. Maruti Esteems and Toyota Qualis are comfortable and have optional reliable air-conditioning. A specialist operator can be very helpful in arranging itineraries and car hire in advance.

Car hire With a driver, car hire is cheaper than in the West. A car shared by three or four can be very good value. Be sure to check carefully the mileage at the beginning and end of the trip. Two- or three-day trips from main towns can also give excellent opportunities for sightseeing off the beaten track in reasonable comfort. Local drivers often know their way much better than drivers from other states, so where possible it is a good idea to get a local driver who speaks the state language, in addition to being able to communicate with you. In the mountains, it is better to use a driver who knows the roads. Drivers may sleep in the car overnight although hotels (especially pricier ones) should provide a bed for them. They are responsible for their expenses, including meals. Car (and auto) drivers increase their earnings by taking you to hotels and shops where they get a handsome commission (which you will pay for). If you feel inclined, a tip at the end of the tour of Rs 100 per day in addition to their daily allowance is perfectly acceptable. Check beforehand if fuel and inter-state taxes are included in the hire charge.

Cars can be hired through private companies. International companies such as **Hertz**, **Europcar** and **Budget** operate in some major cities and offer reliable cars; their rates are generally higher than those of local firms (eg **Sai Service**, **Wheels**). The price of an imported car can be three times that of the Ambassador.

Car with driver	Economy Maruti 800 Ambassador	Regular a/c Maruti 800 Contessa	Premium a/c Maruti 1000 Opel	Luxury a/c Esteem Qualis
8 hrs/80 km	Rs 800	Rs 1000	Rs 1400	Rs 1800+
Extra km	Rs 4-7	Rs 9	Rs 13	Rs 18
Extra hour	Rs 40	Rs 50	Rs 70	Rs 100
Out of town				
Per km	Rs 7	Rs 9	Rs 13	Rs 18
Night halt	Rs 100	Rs 200	Rs 250	Rs 250

Taxi Yellow-top taxis in cities and large towns are metered, although tariffs change frequently. These changes are shown on a fare chart which should be read in conjunction with the meter reading. Increased night time rates apply in some cities, and there is a small charge for luggage. Insist on the taxi meter being flagged in your presence. If the driver refuses, the official advice is to contact the police. This may not work, but it is worth trying. When a taxi doesn't have a meter, you will need to fix the fare before starting the journey. Ask at your hotel desk for a guide price. As a foreigner, it is rare to get a taxi in the big cities to use the meter – if they are eager to, watch out as sometimes the meter is rigged and they have a fake rate card. Also, watch out for the David Blaine-style note shuffle: you pay with a Rs 500 note, but they have a Rs 100 note in their hand. This happens frequently at the pre-paid booth outside New Delhi train station too, no matter how small the transaction.

At stations and airports it is often possible to share taxis to a central point. It is worth looking for fellow passengers who may be travelling in your direction and get a pre-paid taxi. At night, always have a clear idea of where you want to go and insist on being taken there. Taxi drivers may try to convince you that the hotel you have chosen 'closed three years ago' or is 'completely full'. Say that you have a reservation.

Rickshaw **Auto-rickshaws** (autos) are almost universally available in towns across India and are the cheapest and most convenient way of getting about. It is best to walk a short distance away from a hotel gate before picking up an auto to avoid paying an inflated rate. In addition to using them for short journeys it is often possible to hire them by the hour, or for a half or full day's sightseeing. In some areas younger drivers who speak some English and know their local area well may want to show you around. However, rickshaw drivers are often paid a commission by hotels, restaurants and gift shops so advice is not always impartial. Drivers generally refuse to use a meter, often quote a ridiculous price or may sometimes stop short of your destination. If you have real problems it can help to note down the vehicle licence number and threaten to go to the police. Beware of some rickshaw drivers who show the fare chart for taxis, especially in Mumbai.

Cycle-rickshaws and **horse-drawn tongas** are more common in the more rustic setting of a small town or the outskirts of a large one. You will need to fix a price by bargaining. The animal attached to a tonga usually looks too undernourished to have the strength to pull the driver, let alone passengers.

Sleeping

India has an enormous range of accommodation. You can stay safely and very cheaply by Western standards right across the country. In all the major cities there are also high-quality hotels, offering a full range of facilities; in small centres hotels are much more variable. In Rajasthan and Gujarat, old Maharajas' palaces and forts have been privately converted into comfortable, unusual hotels. Hotels in beach resorts and hill stations, because of their location and special appeal, often deviate from the description of our different categories. In the peak season (October to April for most of India) bookings can be extremely heavy in popular destinations. It is sometimes possible to book in advance by phone, fax or email, but double check your reservation, and always try to arrive as early as possible in the day.

Hotels ➔ *For Sleeping price codes, see box, page 15.*

Price categories The category codes used in this book are based on prices of double rooms excluding taxes. They are **not** star ratings and individual facilities vary considerably. The most expensive hotels charge in US dollars only. Modest hotels may not have their own restaurant but will often offer 'room service', bringing in food from outside. In South and West India, and in temple towns, restaurants may only serve vegetarian food. Many hotels operate a 24-hour checkout system. Make sure that this means that you can stay 24 hours from the time of check-in. Expect to pay more in Delhi, Mumbai and, to a lesser extent, in Bengaluru (Bangalore), Chennai and Kolkata for all categories; Kerala, too, is becoming quite expensive. Prices away from large cities tend to be lower for comparable hotels. Away from the metropolitan cities, in South India, room rates tend to be lower than the North, and the standard of cleanliness is higher.

Off-season rates Large reductions are made by hotels in all categories out-of-season in many resorts. Always ask if any is available. You may also request the 10-15% agent's commission to be deducted from your bill if you book direct. Clarify whether the agreed figure includes all taxes.

Taxes In general most hotel rooms rated at Rs 1200 or above are subject to a tax of 10%. Many states levy an additional luxury tax of 10-25%, and some hotels add a service charge

Sleeping and eating price codes

Sleeping

$$$$	over US$150	**$$$**	US$66-150
$$	US$30-65	**$**	Under US$30

For a double room in high season, excluding taxes.

Eating

$$$	over US$12	**$$**	US$6-12	**$**	under US$6

For a two-course meal for one person, excluding drinks and service charge.

of 10% on top of this. Taxes are not necessarily payable on meals, so it is worth settling your meals bill separately. Most hotels in the **$$** category and above accept payment by credit card. Check your final bill carefully. Visitors have complained of incorrect bills, even in the most expensive hotels. The problem particularly afflicts groups, when last-minute extras appear mysteriously on some guests' bills. Check the evening before departure, and keep all receipts.

Hotel facilities You have to be prepared for difficulties which are uncommon in the West. It is best to inspect the room and check that all equipment (air conditioning, TV, water heater, flush) works before checking in at a modest hotel. Many hotels try to wring too many years' service out of their linen, and it's quite common to find sheets that are stained, frayed or riddled with holes. Don't expect any but the most expensive or tourist-savvy hotels to fit a top sheet to the bed.

In some states **power cuts** are common, or hot water may be restricted to certain times of day. The largest hotels have their own generators but it is best to carry a good torch.

In some regions **water supply** is rationed periodically. Keep a bucket filled to use for flushing the toilet during water cuts. Occasionally, tap water may be discoloured due to rusty tanks. During the cold weather and in hill stations, hot water will be available at certain times of the day, sometimes in buckets, but is usually very restricted in quantity. Electric water heaters may provide enough for a shower but not enough to fill a bath tub. For details on drinking water, see page 17.

Hotels close to temples can be very **noisy**, especially during festivals. Music blares from loudspeakers late at night and from very early in the morning, often making sleep impossible. Mosques call the faithful to prayers at dawn. Some find ear plugs helpful.

Homestays

At the upmarket end, increasing numbers of travellers are keen to stay in private homes and guesthouses, opting not to book large hotel chains that keep you at arm's length from a culture. Instead, travellers get home-cooked meals in heritage houses and learn about a country through conversation with often fascinating hosts. Kerala leads the way in this field, but Delhi is catching up fast, with dozens of new and smart family-run B&Bs springing up. Tourist offices have lists of families with more modest homestays. Companies specializing in homestays include **Kerala Connections**, www.kerala connect.co.uk, **MAHout**, www.mahoutuk.com, **Pyramid Tours**, www.pyramidtravel india.com, and **Sundale Vacations**, www.sundale.com.

Eating and drinking → *For Eating price codes, see box, page 15.*

Food

You find as much variety in dishes crossing South India as you would on an equivalent journey across Europe. Combinations of spices give each region its distinctive flavour.

The larger hotels, open to non-residents, often offer **buffet** lunches with Indian, Western and sometimes Chinese dishes. These can be good value (Rs 250-300; but Rs 450 in the top grades) and can provide a welcome, comfortable break in the cool. The health risks, however, of food kept warm for long periods in metal containers are considerable, especially if turnover at the buffet is slow. We have received several complaints of stomach trouble following a buffet meal, even in five-star hotels.

It is essential to be very careful since food hygiene may be poor, flies abound and refrigeration in the hot weather may be inadequate and intermittent because of power cuts. It is best to eat only freshly prepared food by ordering from the menu (especially meat and fish dishes). Avoid salads and cut fruit.

If you are unused to spicy food, go slow. Stick to Western or mild Chinese meals in good restaurants and try the odd Indian dish to test your reaction. Food is often spicier when you eat with families or at local places. Popular local restaurants are obvious from the number of people eating in them. Try a traditional *thali*, which is a complete meal served on a large stainless steel plate (or very occasionally on a banana leaf). Several preparations, placed in small bowls, surround the central serving of wholewheat chapati and rice. A vegetarian *thali* would include dhal (lentils), two or three curries (which can be quite hot) and crisp poppadums, although there are regional variations. A variety of pickles are offered – mango and lime are two of the most popular. These can be exceptionally hot, and are designed to be taken in minute quantities alongside the main dishes. Plain *dahi* (yoghurt) in the south, or *raita* in the north, usually acts as a bland 'cooler'. Simple *dhabas* (rustic roadside eateries) are an alternative experience for sampling authentic local dishes.

Many city restaurants offer a choice of so-called **European options** such as toasted sandwiches, stuffed pancakes, apple pies, fruit crumbles and cheesecakes. Italian favourites (pizzas, pastas) can be very different from what you are used to. In the big cities, Goa and Dharamshala, the Western food is generally pretty good. Western confectionery, in general, is disappointing. **Ice creams**, on the other hand, can be exceptionally good; there are excellent Indian ones as well as some international brands.

India has many delicious tropical **fruits**. Some are seasonal (eg mangoes, pineapples and lychees), while others (eg bananas, grapes and oranges) are available throughout the year. It is safe to eat the ones you can wash and peel.

Despite an abundance of fish and shellfish in Gujarat, Jain and Hindu orthodoxy has encouraged vegetarianism. The Gujarati diet is chiefly rice, wholemeal *chapati*, a variety of beans and pulses rich in protein, and coconut and pickles; a *thali* would include all these, the meal ending with sweetened yoghurt. The dishes themselves are mild, though somewhat sweeter than those of neighbouring states. Popular dishes include: *kadhi*, a savoury yoghurt curry with chopped vegetables and a variety of spices; *undhyoo*, a combination of potatoes, sweet potatoes, aubergines (eggplants) and beans cooked in an earthenware pot in the fire; Surat *paunk* made with tender kernels of millet, sugar balls, savoury twists and garlic chutney. *Ganthia* or *farsan* (light savoury snacks prepared from chickpea and wheat flour), is a regional speciality. Desserts are very sweet. Surat specializes in *gharis* of butter, dried fruit and thickened milk and rich *halwa*. *Srikhand* is saffron-flavoured yoghurt with fruit and nuts.

Drink
Drinking water used to be regarded as one of India's biggest hazards. It is still true that water from the tap or a well should never be considered safe to drink since public water supplies are often polluted. Bottled water is now widely available although not all bottled water is mineral water; most are simply purified water from an urban supply. Buy from a shop or stall, check the seal carefully (some companies now add a second clear plastic seal around the bottle top) and avoid street hawkers; when disposing bottles puncture the neck which prevents misuse but allows recycling.

There is growing concern over the mountains of plastic bottles that are collecting and the waste of resources needed to produce them, so travellers are being encouraged to use alternative methods of getting safe drinking water. A portable water filter is a good idea, carrying the drinking water in a plastic bottle in an insulated carrier. It is important to use pure water for cleaning teeth.

Tea and **coffee** are safe and widely available. Both are normally served sweet, and with milk. If you wish, say 'no sugar' (*chini nahin*), 'no milk' (*dudh nahin*) when ordering. Alternatively, ask for a pot of tea and milk and sugar to be brought separately. Freshly brewed coffee is a common drink in South India, but in the North, ordinary city restaurants will usually serve the instant variety. Even in aspiring smart cafés, espresso or cappuccino may not turn out quite as you'd expect in the West.

Bottled **soft drinks** such as Coke, Pepsi, Teem, Limca, Thums Up and Gold Spot are universally available but always check the seal when you buy from a street stall. There are also several brands of fruit juice sold in cartons, including mango, pineapple and apple – Indian brands are very sweet. Don't add ice cubes as the water source may be contaminated. Take care with fresh fruit juices or *lassis* as ice is often added.

Indians rarely drink **alcohol** with a meal. In the past wines and spirits were generally either imported and extremely expensive, or local and of poor quality. Now, the best Indian whisky, rum and brandy (IMFL or 'Indian Made Foreign Liquor') are widely accepted, as are good Champagnoise and other wines from Maharashtra. If you hanker after a bottle of imported wine, you will only find it in the top restaurants for at least Rs 800-1000.

For the urban elite, refreshing Indian beers are popular when eating out and so are widely available. 'Pubs' have sprung up in the major cities. Elsewhere, seedy, all-male drinking dens in the larger cities are best avoided for women travellers, but can make quite an experience otherwise – you will sometimes be locked into cubicles for clandestine drinking. If that sounds unsavoury then head for the better hotel bars instead; prices aren't that steep. In rural India, local rice, palm, cashew or date juice *toddy* and *arak* is deceptively potent. However, the Sikkimese *chhang* makes a pleasant change drunk out of a wooden tankard through a bamboo straw.

Most states, including Gujarat, have alcohol-free dry days or enforce degrees of Prohibition. Some upmarket restaurants may serve beer even if it's not listed, so it's worth asking. In some states there are government approved wine shops where you buy your alcohol through a metal grille. For liquor permits, see pages 30 and 68.

Festivals and events

India has a wealth of festivals with many celebrated nationwide, while others are specific to a particular state or community or even a particular temple. Many fall on different dates each year depending on the Hindu lunar calendar so check with the tourist office.
▶▶ *Local festivals are listed in the Festivals and events section throughout the book.*

The Hindu calendar
Hindus follow two distinct eras: The *Vikrama Samvat* which began in 57 BC and the *Salivahan Saka* which dates from AD 78 and has been the official Indian calendar since 1957. The *Saka* new year starts on 22 March and has the same length as the Gregorian calendar. The 29½ day lunar month with its 'dark' and 'bright' halves based on the new and full moons, are named after 12 constellations, and total a 354-day year. The calendar cleverly has an extra month (*adhik maas*) every 2½ to three years, to bring it in line with the solar year of 365 days coinciding with the Gregorian calendar of the West.

Some major national and regional festivals are listed below. A few count as national holidays: **26 January**: Republic Day; **15 August**: Independence Day; **2 October**: Mahatma Gandhi's Birthday; **25 December**: Christmas Day.

Major festivals and fairs

Jan New Year's Day (**1 Jan**) is accepted officially when following the Gregorian calendar but there are regional variations which fall on different dates, often coinciding with spring/harvest time in Mar and Apr.
14 Jan Makar Sankranti marks the end of winter and is celebrated with kite flying.
Feb Vasant Panchami, the spring festival when people wear bright yellow clothes to mark the advent of the season with singing, dancing and feasting.
Feb-Mar Maha Sivaratri marks the night when Siva danced his celestial dance of destruction (*Tandava*), which is celebrated with feasting and fairs at Siva temples, but preceded by a night of devotional readings and hymn singing.
Mar Holi, the festival of colours, marks the climax of spring. The previous night bonfires are lit symbolizing the end of winter (and conquering of evil). People have fun throwing coloured powder and water at each other and in the evening some gamble with friends. If you don't mind getting covered in colours, you can risk going out

but celebrations can sometimes get very rowdy (and unpleasant). Some worship Krishna who defeated the demon Putana.
Apr/May Buddha Jayanti, the 1st full moon night in Apr/May marks the birth of the Buddha.
Jul/Aug Raksha (or Rakhi) Bandhan symbolizes the bond between brother and sister, celebrated at full moon. A sister says special prayers for her brother and ties coloured threads around his wrist to remind him of the special bond. He in turn gives a gift and promises to protect and care for her. Sometimes *rakshas* are exchanged as a mark of friendship. **Narial Purnima** on the same full moon. Hindus make offerings of *narial* (coconuts) to the Vedic god Varuna (Lord of the waters) by throwing them into the sea.
15 Aug is **Independence Day**, a national secular holiday is marked by special events.
Ganesh Chaturthi was established just over 100 years ago by the Indian nationalist leader Tilak. The elephant-headed God of good omen is shown special reverence. On the last of the 5-day festival after harvest, clay

images of Ganesh are taken in procession with dancers and musicians, and are immersed in the sea, river or pond.

Aug/Sep Janmashtami, the birth of Krishna is celebrated at midnight at Krishna temples.

Sep/Oct Dasara has many local variations. Celebrations for the 9 nights *(navaratri)* are marked with **Ramlila**, various episodes of the Ramayana story are enacted with particular reference to the battle between the forces of good and evil. In some parts of India it celebrates *Rama's* victory over the Demon king *Ravana* of Lanka with the help of loyal *Hanuman* (Monkey). Huge effigies of *Ravana* made of bamboo and paper are burnt on the 10th day (*Vijaya dasami*) of **Dasara** in public open spaces. In other regions the focus is on Durga's victory over the demon *Mahishasura*.

Oct/Nov Gandhi Jayanti (**2 Oct**), Mahatma Gandhi's birthday, is remembered with prayer meetings and devotional singing.

Diwali/Deepavali (*Sanskrit ideepa* lamp), the festival of lights, is celebrated particularly in North India. Some Hindus celebrate Krishna's victory over the demon *Narakasura*, some Rama's return after his 14 years' exile in the forest when citizens lit his way with oil lamps. The festival falls on the dark *chaturdasi* (14th) night (the one preceding the new moon), when rows of lamps or candles are lit in remembrance, and *rangolis* are painted on the floor as a sign of welcome. Fireworks have become an integral part of the celebration which are often set off days before Diwali. Equally, Lakshmi, the Goddess of Wealth (as well as Ganesh) is worshipped by merchants and the business community who open the new financial year's account on the day. Most people wear new clothes; some play games of chance.

Guru Nanak Jayanti commemorates the birth of Guru Nanak. **Akhand Path** (unbroken reading of the holy book) takes place and the book itself (*Guru Granth Sahib*) is taken out in procession.

Dec Christmas Day (**25 Dec**) sees Indian Christians celebrate the birth of Christ in much the same way as in the West; many churches hold services/mass at midnight. There is an air of festivity in city markets which are specially decorated and illuminated. Over **New Year's Eve** (**31 Dec**) hotel prices peak and large supplements are added for meals and entertainment in the upper category hotels. Some churches mark the night with a Midnight Mass.

Muslim holy days

These are fixed according to the lunar calendar. According to the Gregorian calendar, they tend to fall 11 days earlier each year, dependent on the sighting of the new moon.

Ramadan is the start of the month of fasting when all Muslims (except young children, the very elderly, the sick, pregnant women and travellers) must abstain from food and drink, from sunrise to sunset.

Id ul Fitr is the 3-day festival that marks the end of Ramadan.

Id-ul-Zuha/Bakr-Id is when Muslims commemorate Ibrahim's sacrifice of his son according to God's commandment; the main time of pilgrimage to Mecca (the Hajj). It is marked by the sacrifice of a goat, feasting and alms giving.

Muharram is when the killing of the Prophet's grandson, Hussain, is commemorated by Shi'a Muslims. Decorated *tazias* (replicas of the martyr's tomb) are carried in procession by devout wailing followers who beat their chests to express their grief. Hyderabad and Lucknow are famous for their grand *tazias*. Shi'as fast for the 10 days.

Responsible travel

As well as respecting local cultural sensitivities, travellers can take a number of simple steps to reduce, or even improve, their impact on the local environment. Environmental concern is relatively new in India. Don't be afraid to pressurize businesses by asking about their policies.

Litter Many travellers think that there is little point in disposing of rubbish properly when the tossing of water bottles, plastic cups and other non-biodegradable items out of train windows is already so widespread. Don't follow an example you feel to be wrong. You can immediately reduce your impact by refusing plastic bags and other excess packaging when shopping – use a small backpack or cloth bag instead – and if you do collect a few, keep them with you to store other rubbish until you get to a litter bin.

Plastic mineral water bottles, an inevitable corollary to poor water hygiene standards, are a major contributor to India's litter mountain. However, many hotels, including nearly all of the upmarket ones, most restaurants and bus and train stations, provide drinking water purified using a combination of ceramic and carbon filters, chlorine and UV irradiation. Ask for *'filter paani'*; if the water tastes like a swimming pool it is probably quite safe to drink, though it's best to introduce your body gradually to the new water. If purifying water yourself, bringing it to a boil at sea level will make it safe, but at altitude you have to boil it for longer to ensure that all the microbes are killed. Various sterilizing methods can be used that contain chlorine (eg Puritabs) or iodine (eg Pota Aqua) and there are a number of mechanical or chemical water filters available on the market.

Bucket baths or showers The biggest issue relating to responsible and sustainable tourism is water. Much of northwest India is afflicted by severe water restrictions, with certain cities in Rajasthan and Gujarat having water supply for as little as 20 minutes a day. The traditional Indian 'bucket bath', in which you wet, soap then rinse off using a small hand-held plastic jug dipped into a large bucket, uses on average around 15 litres of water, as compared to 30-45 for a shower. These are commonly offered except in four- and five-star hotels.

Support responsible tourism Spending your money carefully can have a positive impact. Sleeping, eating and shopping at small, locally owned businesses directly supports communities, while specific community tourism concerns, such as those operated by The **Blue Yonder** in Kerala and **Village Ways** in Uttarakhand, provide an economic motivation for people to stay in remote communities, protect natural areas and revive traditional cultures, rather than exploit the environment or move to the cities for work.

Transport Choose walking, cycling or public transport over fuel-guzzling cars and motorbikes.

Essentials A-Z

Accident and emergency

Contact the relevant emergency service (police T100, fire T101, ambulance T102) and your embassy (see under Directory in major cities). Make sure you obtain police/medical reports required for insurance claims.

Customs and duty free
Duty free

Tourists are allowed to bring in all personal effects 'which may reasonably be required', without charge. The official customs allowance includes 200 cigarettes or 50 cigars, 0.95 litres of alcohol, a camera and a pair of binoculars. Valuable personal effects and professional equipment including jewellery, special camera equipment and lenses, laptop computers and sound and video recorders must be declared on a Tourist Baggage Re-Export Form (TBRE) in order for them to be taken out of the country. These forms require the equipment's serial numbers. It saves considerable frustration if you know the numbers in advance and are ready to show them on the equipment. In addition to the forms, details of imported equipment may be entered into your passport. Save time by completing the formalities while waiting for your baggage. It is essential to keep these forms for showing to the customs when leaving India, otherwise considerable delays are very likely at the time of departure.

Prohibited items

The import of dangerous drugs, live plants, gold coins, gold and silver bullion and silver coins not in current use are either banned or subject to strict regulation. It is illegal to import firearms into India without special permission. Enquire at consular offices abroad for details.

Drugs

Certain areas, such as Goa's beaches, Kovalam, Gokarna and Hampi, have become associated with foreigners who take drugs. These are likely to attract local and foreign drug dealers but be aware that the government takes the misuse of drugs very seriously. Anyone charged with the illegal possession of drugs risks facing a fine of Rs 100,000 and a minimum 10 years' imprisonment. Several foreigners have been imprisoned for drugs-related offences in the last decade.

Electricity

Inida supply is 220-240 volts AC. Some top hotels have transformers. There may be pronounced variations in the voltage, and power cuts are common. Power back-up by generator or inverter is becoming more widespread, even in humble hotels, though it may not cover a/c. Socket sizes vary so take a universal adaptor; low-quality versions are available locally. Many hotels, even in the higher categories, don't have electric razor sockets. Invest in a stabilizer for a laptop.

Embassies and consulates

For information on visas and immigration, see page 29. For a comprehensive list of embassies (but not all consulates), see http://india.gov.in/ overseas/indian_missions.php. Many embassies around the world are now outsourcing the visa process which might affect how long the process takes.

Health

Local populations in India are exposed to a range of health risks not encountered in the Western world. Many of the diseases are major problems for the local poor and destitute and, although the risk to travellers is more remote, they cannot be ignored. Obviously 5-star travel is going to carry less risk than backpacking on a budget.

Health care in the region is varied. There are many excellent private and government clinics/hospitals. As with all medical care, first impressions count. It's worth contacting your embassy or consulate on arrival and asking where the recommended (ie those used by diplomats) clinics are. You can also ask about locally recommended medical do's and don'ts. If you do get ill, and you have the opportunity, you should also ask your medical insurer whether they are satisfied that the medical centre/hospital you have been referred to is of a suitable standard.

Before you go

Ideally, you should see your GP or travel clinic at least 6 weeks before your departure for general advice on travel risks, malaria and vaccinations. Make sure you have travel insurance, get a dental check (especially if you are going to be away for more than a month), know your own blood group and if you suffer a long-term condition such as diabetes or epilepsy make sure someone knows or that you have a Medic Alert bracelet/necklace with this information on it. Remember that it is risky to buy medicinal tablets abroad because the doses may differ and India has a huge trade in false drugs.

Vaccinations

If you need vaccinations, see your doctor well in advance of your travel. Most courses must be completed by a minimum of 4 weeks. Travel clinics may provide rapid courses of vaccination, but are likely to be more expensive. The following vaccinations are recommended: typhoid, polio, tetanus, infectious hepatitis and diptheria. For details of malaria prevention, contact your GP or local travel clinic.

The following vaccinations may also be considered: rabies, possibly BCG (since TB is still common in the region) and in some cases meningitis and diphtheria (if you're staying in the country for a long time). Yellow fever is not required in India but you may be asked to show a certificate if you have travelled from Africa or South America. Japanese encephalitis may be required for rural travel at certain times of the year (mainly rainy seasons). An effective oral cholera vaccine (Dukoral) is now available as 2 doses providing 3 months' protection.

Websites

Blood Care Foundation (UK), www.bloodcare.org.uk A Kent-based charity 'dedicated to the provision of screened blood and resuscitation fluids in countries where these are not readily available'. They will dispatch certified non-infected blood of the right type to your hospital/clinic. The blood is flown in from various centres around the world.
British Travel Health Association (UK), www.btha.org This is the official website of an organization of travel health professionals.
Fit for Travel, www.fitfortravel.scot. nhs.uk This site from Scotland provides a quick A-Z of vaccine and travel health advice requirements for each country.
Foreign and Commonwealth Office (FCO) (UK), www.fco.gov.uk This is a key travel advice site, with useful information on the country, people, climate and lists the UK embassies/consulates. The site also promotes the concept of 'know before you go' and encourages travel insurance and appropriate travel health advice. It has links to Department of Health travel advice site.
The Health Protection Agency, www.hpa. org.uk Up-to-date malaria advice guidelines for travel around the world. It gives specific advice about the right drugs for each location. It also has useful information for those who are

pregnant, suffering from epilepsy or planning to travel with children.

Medic Alert (UK), www.medicalalert.com This is the website of the foundation that produces bracelets and necklaces for those with existing medical problems. Once you have ordered your bracelet/necklace you write your key medical details on paper inside it, so that if you collapse, a medic can identify you as having epilepsy or a nut allergy, etc.

Travel Screening Services (UK), www.travelscreening.co.uk A private clinic dedicated to integrated travel health. The clinic gives vaccine, travel health advice, email and SMS text vaccine reminders and screens returned travellers for tropical diseases.

World Health Organisation, www.who. int The WHO site has links to the *WHO Blue Book* on travel advice. This lists the diseases in different regions of the world. It describes vaccination schedules and makes clear which countries have yellow fever vaccination certificate requirements and malarial risk.

Books

International Travel and Health World Health Organisation Geneva, ISBN 92-4-15802-6-7.

Lankester, T, *The Travellers Good Health Guide*, ISBN 0-85969-827-0.

Warrell, D and Anderson, A (eds), *Expedition Medicine (The Royal Geographic Society)*, ISBN 1-86197-040-4.

Young Pelton, R, Aral, C and Dulles, W, *The World's Most Dangerous Places*, ISBN 1-566952-140-9.

Language

Hindi, spoken as a mother tongue by over 400 million people, is India's official language. The use of English is also enshrined in the Constitution for a wide range of official purposes, notably communication between Hindi and non-Hindi speaking states. The most widely spoken Indo-Aryan languages are: Bengali (8.3%), Marathi (8%), Urdu (5.7%), Gujarati (5.4%), Oriya (3.7%) and Punjabi

(3.2%). Among the Dravidian languages Telugu (8.2%), Tamil (7%), Kannada (4.2%) and Malayalam (3.5%) are the most widely used. Most people in Gujarat speak Gujarati, an Indo-Ayran language of Sanskrit origin but with some Persian, Arabic, Portuguese and English vocabulary deriving from maritime contacts. About 15% of the state's population is tribal.

English now plays an important role across India. It is widely spoken in towns and cities and even in quite remote villages it is usually not difficult to find someone who speaks at least a little English. Outside of major tourist sites, other European languages are almost completely unknown. The accent in which English is spoken is often affected strongly by the mother tongue of the speaker and there have been changes in common grammar which sometimes make it sound unusual. Many of these changes have become standard Indian English usage, as valid as any other varieties of English used around the world. It is possible to study a number of Indian languages at language centres.

Money

Indian currency is the Indian Rupee (Re/Rs). It is **not** possible to purchase these before you arrive. If you want cash on arrival it is best to get it at the airport bank, although see if an ATM is available as airport rates are not very generous. Rupee notes are printed in denominations of Rs 1000, 500, 100, 50, 20, 10. The rupee is divided into 100 paise. Coins are minted in denominations of Rs 5, Rs 2, Rs 1 and 50 paise. **Note** Carry money, mostly as traveller's cheques, in a money belt worn under clothing. Have a small amount in an easily accessible place.

Exchange rates *(Sep 2011)*

UK £1 = Rs 73.9, €1 = Rs 64.7, US$1 = Rs 46

Traveller's cheques (TCs)

TCs issued by reputable companies (eg **Thomas Cook**, **American Express**) are widely accepted. They can be easily exchanged at small local travel agents and tourist internet cafés but are rarely used directly for payment. Try to avoid changing at banks, where the process can be time consuming; opt for hotels and agents instead, take large denomination cheques and change enough to last for some days. Most banks, but not all, will accept US dollars, pounds sterling and euro TCs so it is a good idea to carry some of each. Other major currency TCs are also accepted in some larger cities. One traveller warns that replacement of lost Amex TCs may take weeks. If travelling to remote areas it can be worth buying Indian rupee TCs from a major bank, these are more widely accepted than foreign currency ones.

Credit cards

Major credit cards are increasingly acceptable in the main centres, though in smaller cities and towns it is still rare to be able to pay by credit card. Payment by credit card can sometimes be more expensive than payment by cash, whilst some credit card companies charge a premium on cash withdrawals. **Visa** and **MasterCard** have a growing number of ATMs in major cities and several banks offer withdrawal facilities for Cirrus and Maestro cardholders. It is however easy to obtain a cash advance against a credit card. Railway reservation centres in major cities take payment for train tickets by Visa card which can be very quick as the queue is short, although they cannot be used for Tourist Quota tickets.

ATMs

By far the most convenient method of accessing money, ATMs are all over India, usually attended by security guards, with most banks offering some services to holders of overseas cards. Banks whose ATMs will issue cash against Cirrus and Maestro cards, as well as Visa and MasterCard, include

Bank of Baroda, Citibank, HDFC, HSBC, ICICI, IDBI, Punjab National Bank, State Bank of India (SBI), Standard Chartered and UTI. A withdrawal fee is usually charged by the issuing bank on top of the conversion charges applied by your own bank. Fraud prevention measures quite often result in travellers having their cards blocked by the bank when unexpected overseas transactions occur; advise your bank of your travel plans before leaving.

Changing money

The **State Bank of India** and several others in major towns are authorized to deal in foreign exchange. Some give cash against Visa/MasterCard (eg **ANZ**, **Bank of Baroda** who print a list of their participating branches, **Andhra Bank**). American Express cardholders can use their cards to get either cash or TCs in Mumbai and Chennai. They also have offices in Coimbatore, Goa, Hyderabad, and Thiruvananthapuram. The larger cities have licensed money changers with offices usually in the commercial sector. Changing money through unauthorized dealers is illegal. Premiums on the currency black market are very small and highly risky. Large hotels change money 24 hrs a day for guests, but banks often give a substantially better rate of exchange. It is best to exchange money on arrival at the airport bank or the Thomas Cook counter. Many international flights arrive during the night and it is generally far easier and less time consuming to change money at the airport than in the city. You should be given a foreign currency encashment certificate when you change money through a bank or authorized dealer; ask for one if it is not automatically given. It allows you to change Indian rupees back to your own currency on departure. It also enables you to use rupees to pay hotel bills or buy air tickets for which payment in foreign exchange may be required. The certificates are only valid for 3 months.

Cost of living

The cost of living in India remains well below that in the West. The average wage per capita is about Rs 34,000 per year (US$800). Manual, unskilled labourers (women are often paid less than men), farmers and others in rural areas earn considerably less. However, thanks to booming global demand for workers who can provide cheaper IT and technology support functions and many Western firms transferring office functions or call centres to India, salaries in certain sectors have sky rocketed. An IT specialist can earn an average Rs 500,000 per year and upwards – a rate that is rising by around 15% a year.

Cost of travelling

Most food, accommodation and public transport, especially rail and bus, is exceptionally cheap, although inflation in 2010 was 16.3% and basic food items such as rice, lentils, tomatoes and onions have skyrocketed. There is a widening range of moderately priced but clean hotels and restaurants outside the big cities, making it possible to get a great deal for your money. Budget travellers sharing a room, taking public transport, avoiding souvenir stalls, and eating nothing but rice and dhal can get away with a budget of Rs 400-600 (about US$8-12 or £5-8) a day. This sum leaps up if you drink alcohol (still cheap by European standards at about US$2, £1 or Rs 80 for a pint), smoke foreign-brand cigarettes or want to have your own wheels (you can expect to spend between Rs 150 and 200 to hire a Honda per day). Those planning to stay in fairly comfortable hotels and use taxis sightseeing should budget at US$50-80 (£30-50) a day. Then again you could always check into **Ananda Spa** or the **Taj Falaknuma** for Christmas and notch up an impressive US$600 (£350) bill on your B&B alone. India can be a great place to pick and choose, save a little on basic accommodation and then treat yourself to the type of meal you could only dream of affording back home. Also, be prepared to spend a fair amount more in Mumbai, Hyderabad, Bengaluru (Bangalore) and Chennai, where not only is the cost of living significantly higher but where it's worth coughing up extra for a half-decent room: penny-pinch by the beach when you'll be spending precious little time indoors anyway. A newspaper costs Rs 5 and breakfast for 2 with coffee can come to as little as Rs 50 in a South Indian 'hotel', but if you intend to eat banana pancakes or pasta beside a Goan beach, you can expect to pay more like Rs 50-150 a plate.

Opening hours

Banks are open Mon-Fri 1030-1430, Sat 1030-1230. Top hotels sometimes have a 24-hr money changing service. **Post offices** open Mon-Fri 1000-1700, often shutting for lunch, and Sat mornings. **Government offices** Mon-Fri 0930-1700, Sat 0930-1300 (some open on alternate Sat only). **Shops** open Mon-Sat 0930-1800. Bazars keep longer hours.

Post

The post is frequently unreliable, and delays are common. It is best to use a post office where you can hand over mail for franking across the counter, or a top hotel post box. Valuable items should only be sent by registered mail. Government emporia or shops in the larger hotels will send purchases home if the items are difficult to carry. Seamail and Book Post have been on hold since Jan 2008 because of the Somali pirate situation – best to check for availability.

Airmail services to Europe, Africa and Australia take at least a week and a little longer for the Americas. **Speed post** (which takes about 4 days to the UK) is available from major towns. Speed post to the UK from Tamil Nadu costs Rs 675 for the first 250g sent and an extra Rs 75 for each 250g thereafter. **Courier services** (eg DHL) are available in the larger towns. At some main post offices you can send small packages under 2 kg as **letter post** (rather than parcel post), which is much cheaper at Rs 220. Check that the post office holds necessary customs declaration forms (2-3 copies needed). Write 'No commercial value' if returning used clothes, books, etc. **Sea mail** costs Rs 800 for 10 kg. 'Packers' at or near the post office do necessary cloth covering, sealing, etc for Rs 20-50; you address the parcel, obtain stamps from a separate counter; stick stamps and a customs form to the parcel with the provided glue (the other form/s must be partially sewn on). Post at the Parcels Counter and obtain a registration slip. Cost varies by destination and is normally displayed on a board beside the counter. Specialist shippers deal with larger items, normally around US$150 per cubic metre. Sea mail is currently being phased out to be replaced by **SAL** (Surface Air Lifted). The prices are fractionally lower than airmail, Rs 500-600 for the first kg and Rs 150-250 per extra kg. Delivery can take up to 2 months.

Poste Restante facilities are widely available in even quite small towns at the GPO where mail is held for 1 month. Ask for mail to be addressed to you with your surname in capitals and underlined. When asking for mail at Poste Restante check under surname as well as christian name.

Safety
Personal security

In general the threats to personal security for travellers in India are remarkably small. However, incidents of petty theft and violence directed specifically at tourists have been on the increase so care is necessary in some places, and basic common sense needs to be used with respect to looking after valuables. Follow the same precautions you would when at home. There have been incidents of sexual assault in and around the main tourist beach centres, particularly after full moon parties in South India. Avoid wandering alone outdoors late at night in these places. During daylight hours be careful in remote places, especially when alone. If you are under threat, scream loudly. Be very cautious before accepting food or drink from casual acquaintances, as it may be drugged.

The left-wing Maoist extremist Naxalites are active in east central and southern India. They have a long history of conflict with state and national authorities, including attacks on police and government officials. The Naxalites have not specifically targeted Westerners, but have attacked symbolic targets including Western companies. As a general rule, travellers are advised to be vigilant in the lead up to and on days of national significance, such as Republic Day (26 Jan) and Independence Day (15 Aug) as militants have in the past used such occasions to mount attacks.

Following a major explosion on the Delhi to Lahore (Pakistan) train in Feb 2007 and the Mumbai attacks in Nov 2008, increased security has been implemented on many trains and stations. Similar measures at airports may cause delays for passengers so factor this into your timing. Also check your airline's website for up-to-date information on luggage restrictions. In Mumbai, the UK's Foreign and Commonwealth Office warns of a risk of armed robbers holding up taxis travelling along the main highway from the airport to the city in the early hours of the morning (0200-0600) when there is little traffic on the roads. If you are using the route during these times, you should, if possible, arrange to travel by coach or seek advice at the airport on arrival.

That said, in the great majority of places visited by tourists, violent crime and personal attacks are extremely rare.

Travel advice

It is better to seek advice from your consulate than from travel agencies. Before you travel you can contact: **British Foreign & Common-wealth Office Travel Advice Unit**, T0845-850 2829 (Pakistan desk T020-7270 2385), www.fco.gov.uk. **US State Department's Bureau of Consular Affairs**, Overseas Citizens Services, Room 4800, Department of State, Washington, DC 20520-4818, USA, T202-647 1488, http://travel.state.gov. **Australian Department of Foreign Affairs Canberra**, Australia, T02-6261 3305, www.smartraveller.gov.au. Canadian official advice is on www.voyage.gc.ca.

Theft

Theft is not uncommon. It is best to keep TCs, passports and valuables with you at all times. Don't regard hotel rooms as being automatically safe; even hotel safes don't guarantee secure storage. Avoid leaving valuables near open windows even when you are in the room. Use your own padlock in a budget hotel when you go out. Pickpockets and other thieves operate in the big cities. Crowded areas are particularly high risk. Take special care of your belongings when getting on or off public transport.

If you have items stolen, they should be reported to the police as soon as possible. Keep a separate record of vital documents, including passport details and numbers of TCs. Larger hotels will be able to assist in contacting and dealing with the police. Dealings with the police can be very difficult and in the worst regions, such as Bihar, even dangerous. The paperwork involved in reporting losses can be time consuming and irritating and your own documentation (eg passport and visas) may be demanded.

In some states the police occasionally demand bribes, though you should not assume that if procedures move slowly you are automatically being expected to offer a bribe. The traffic police are tightening up on traffic offences in some places. They have the right to make on-the-spot fines for speeding and illegal parking. If you face a fine, insist on a receipt. If you have to go to a police station, try to take someone with you.

If you face really serious problems (eg in connection with a driving accident), contact your consular office as quickly as possible. You should ensure you always have your international driving licence and motorbike or car documentation with you.

Confidence tricksters are particularly common where people are on the move, notably around railway stations or places where budget tourists gather. A common plea is some sudden and desperate calamity; sometimes a letter will be produced in English to back up the claim. The demands are likely to increase sharply if sympathy is shown.

Telephone

The international code for India is +91. International Direct Dialling is widely available in privately run call booths, usually labelled on yellow boards with the letters 'PCO-STD-ISD'. You dial the call yourself, and the time and cost are displayed on a computer screen. Cheap rate (2100-0600) means long queues may form outside booths. Telephone calls from hotels are usually more expensive (check price before calling), though some will allow local calls free of charge. Internet phone booths, usually associated with cybercafés, are the cheapest way of calling overseas.

A double ring repeated regularly means it is ringing; equal tones with equal pauses means engaged (similar to the UK). If calling a mobile, rather than ringing, you might hear music while you wait for an answer.

One disadvantage of the tremendous pace of the telecommunications revolution is the fact that millions of telephone numbers go out of date every year. Current telephone directories themselves are often out of date and some of the numbers given in this book will have been changed even as we go to press. Our best advice is if the number in the text does not work, add a '2'. **Directory enquiries**, T197, can be helpful but works only for the local area code.

Mobile phones are for sale everywhere, as are local SIM cards that allow you to make calls within India and overseas at much lower rates than using a 'roaming' service from your normal provider at home – sometimes for as little as Rs 0.5 per min. Arguably the best service is provided by the government carrier **BSNL/MTNL** but security provisions make connecting to the service virtually impossible for foreigners. Private companies such as **Airtel**, **Vodafone**, **Reliance** and **Tata Indicom** are easier to sign up with, but the deals they offer can be befuddling and are frequently changed. To connect you'll need to complete a form, have a local address or receipt showing the address of your hotel, and present photocopies of your passport and visa plus 2 passport photos to an authorized reseller – most phone dealers will be able to help, and can also sell top-up. **Univercell**, www.univercell.in, and **The Mobile Store**, www.themobilestore.in, are 2 widespread and efficient chains selling phones and sim cards.

India is divided into a number of 'calling circles' or regions, and if you travel outside the region where your connection is based, eg from Delhi into Rajasthan, you will pay higher charges for making and receiving calls, and any problems that may occur – with 'unverified' documents, for example – can be much harder to resolve.

Time
India doesn't change its clocks, so from the last Sun in Oct to the last Sun in Mar the time is GMT +5½ hrs, and the rest of the year it's +4½ hrs (USA, EST +10½ and +9½ hrs; Australia, EST -5½ and -4½ hrs).

Tipping
A tip of Rs 10 to a bellboy carrying luggage in a modest hotel (Rs 20 in a higher category) would be appropriate. In upmarket restaurants, a 10% tip is acceptable when service is not already included, while in places serving very cheap meals, round off the bill with small change. Indians don't normally tip taxi drivers but a small extra is welcomed. Porters at airports and railway stations often have a fixed rate displayed but will usually press for more. Ask fellow passengers what a fair rate is.

Tourist information
There are **Government of India** tourist offices in the state capitals, as well as state tourist offices (sometimes **Tourism Development Corporations**) in the major cities and a few important sites. They produce their own tourist literature, either free or sold at a nominal price, and some also have lists of city hotels and paying guest options. The quality of material is improving though maps are often poor. Many offer tours of the city, neighbouring sights and overnight and regional packages. Some run modest hotels and midway motels with restaurants and may also arrange car hire and guides. The staff in the regional and local offices are usually helpful.

Tourist offices overseas
Australia Level 5, Glasshouse,135 King St, Sydney, NSW 2000, T02-9221 9555, info@ indiatourism.com.au.
Canada 60 Bloor St West, Suite No 1003, Toronto, Ontario, T416-962 3787, indiatourism@bellnet.ca.
Dubai 6 Post Box 12856, NASA Building, Al Maktoum Rd, Deira, T04-227 4848, goirto@emirates.net.ae.
France 11-13 Bis Blvd Hausmann, 75009, Paris T01-4523 3045.
Germany Baserler St 48, 60329, Frankfurt AM-Main 1, T069-242 9490, www.india-tourism.de.

Italy Via Albricci 9, Milan 20122,
T02-805 3506, info@indiatourismmilan.com.
Japan B9F Chiyoda Building, 1-8-17 Ginza,
Chuo-Ku, Tokyo 104-0061, T03-3561 0651,
indiatourt@smile.ocn.ne.jp.
The Netherlands Rokin 9-15,
1012 KK Amsterdam, T020-620 8991,
info@indiatourismamsterdam.com.
Singapore 20 Kramat Lane, 01-01A United
House, 228773, Singapore, T6235-3800,
indtour.sing@pacific.net.sg.
South Africa Hyde Lane,
Lancaster Gate, Johannesburg,
T011-325 0880, goito@global.co.za.
UK 7 Cork St, London WIS 3LH,
T020-74373677, T08700-102183,
london5@indiatouristoffice.org.
USA 3550 Wilshire Blvd, Room 204, Los
Angeles, California 90010, T213-380 8855,
goitola@aol.com; Suite 1808, 1270 Av
of Americas, New York, NY 10020-1700,
T212-5864901, ny@itonyc.com.
Also check out www.incredibleindia.org
for information.

Visas and immigration

For embassies and consulates, see page 21.
Virtually all foreign nationals, including
children, require a visa to enter India.
Nationals of Bhutan and Nepal only require
a suitable means of identification. The rules
regarding visas change frequently and
arrangements for application and collection
also vary from town to town so it is essential
to check details and costs with the relevant
embassy or consulate. These remain closed
on Indian national holidays. Now many
consulates and embassies are outsourcing
the visa process, it's best to find out in
advance how long it will take. For example,
in London where you used to be able to get
a visa in person in a morning if you were
prepared to queue, it now takes 2-3 working
days and involves 2 trips to the office.

At other offices, it can be much easier to
apply in advance by post, to avoid queues
and frustratingly low visa quotas. Postal
applications can 15 working days to process.

Visitors from countries with no Indian
representation may apply to the resident
British representative, or enquire at the
Air India office. An application on the
prescribed form should be accompanied by
2 passport photographs and your passport
which should be valid 6 months beyond the
period of your visit. Note that visas are valid
from the date granted, not from the date
of entry. For up-to-date information on visa
requirements visit www.india-visa.com.

No foreigner needs to register within the
180-day period of their tourist visa. All foreign
visitors who stay in India for more than
180 days need to get an income tax clearance
exemption certificate from the Foreign
Section of the Income Tax Department in
Delhi, Mumbai, Kolkata or Chennai.

Currently the following visa rules apply:
Transit For passengers en route to another
country (no more than 72 hrs in India).
Tourist Normally valid for 3-6 months from
date of issue, though some nationalities may
be granted visas for up to 5 years. Multiple
entries permitted, but a new rule requires a
2-month wait before you can return to India.
The rule doesn't apply if you plan to visit
neighbouring countries as part of your trip
(eg Nepal, Sri Lanka), but you need clear
documentation proving your itinerary.
Business 3-6 months or up to 2 years with
multiple entry. A letter from the company
giving the nature of business is required.
5 year For those of Indian origin only,
who have held Indian passports.
Student Valid up to 1 year from the date
of issue. Attach a letter of acceptance from
Indian institution and an AIDS test certificate.
Allow up to 3 months for approval.
Visa extensions Applications should be
made to the Foreigners' Regional Registration
Offices at New Delhi, Mumbai, Kolkata or
Chennai, or an office of the Superintendent
of Police in the District Headquarters. After

6 months, you must leave India and apply for a new visa – the Nepal office is known to be difficult. Anyone staying in India for a period of more than 180 days (6 months) must register at a convenient Foreigners' Registration Office.

Work permits
Foreigners should apply to the Indian representative in their country of origin for the latest information about work permits.

Liquor permits
Periodically some Indian states have tried to enforce prohibition. To some degree it is in force in Gujarat, Manipur, Mizoram and Nagaland. When applying for your visa you can ask for an All India Liquor Permit. Foreigners can also get the permit from any Government of India Tourist Office in Delhi or the state capitals. Instant permits are issued by some hotels.

Weights and measures
Metric is in universal use in the cities. In remote areas local measures are sometimes used. One lakh is 100,000 and 1 crore is 10 million.

Women travellers
Independent travel is still largely unheard of for Indian women. Although it is relatively safe for women to travel around India, most people find it an advantage to travel with a companion. Even then, privacy is rarely respected and there can be a lot of hassle, pressure and intrusion on your personal space, as well as some outright harassment. Backpackers setting out alone often meet like-minded travelling companions at budget hotels. Cautious women travellers recommend dying blonde hair black and wearing wedding rings, but the most important measure to ensure respect is to dress appropriately, in loose-fitting, non-see-through clothes, covering shoulders, arms and legs (such as a *salwaar kameez*, which can be made to fit in around 24 hrs for around Rs 400-800). Take advantage, too, of the gender segregation on public transport, to avoid hassle and to talk to local women. In mosques women should be covered from head to ankle.

Independent Traveller, T0870-760 5001, www.independenttraveller.com, runs women-only tours to India.

'Eve teasing', the euphemism for physical harassment, is an unfortunate result of the sexual repression latent in Indian culture, combined with a young male population whose only access to sex education is via the dingy cybercafés. Unaccompanied women are most vulnerable in major cities, crowded bazars, beach resorts and tourist centres where men may follow them and touch them; festival nights are particularly bad for this. Women have reported that they have been molested while being measured for clothing in tailors' shops. If you are harassed, it can be effective to make a scene. Be firm and clear if you don't wish to speak to someone. The best response to staring, whether lascivious or curious, is to avert your eyes down and away. This is not the submissive gesture it might seem, but an effective tool to communicate that you have no interest in any further interaction. Aggressively staring back or confronting the starer can be construed as a come-on. It is best to be accompanied at night, especially when travelling by rickshaw or taxi in towns. Be prepared to raise an alarm if anything unpleasant threatens.

Most railway booking offices have separate women's ticket queues or ask women to go to the head of the general queue. Some buses have seats reserved for women.

Contents

Footprint features

At a glance

⊖ **Getting around** Ride the suburban railway network in Mumbai, the narrow gauge up to Matheran and the Konkan railway out of state. In Mumbai cabs and motor rickshaws are plentiful.

⏱ **Time required** Allow 48 hrs for Mumbai, 2 days for Ajanta and Ellora.

☁ **Weather** Hot all year, with a heavy monsoon.

✖ **When not to go** Jun and Jul when rainfall is torrential.

Mumbai & around

Mumbai (Bombay)

From the cluster of fishing villages first linked together by the British East India Company in 1668, Mumbai has swelled to sprawl across seven islands, which now groan under the needs of 19 million stomachs, souls and egos. Its problems – creaking infrastructure, endemic corruption coupled with bureaucratic incompetence, and an ever-expanding population of whom more than two thirds live in slums – are only matched by the enormous drive that makes it the centre of business, fashion and film-making in modern India, and both a magnet and icon for the country's dreams, and nightmares.

The taxi ride from the airport shows you both sides of the city: slum dwellers selling balloons under billboards of fair-skinned models dripping in gold and reclining on the roof of a Mercedes; the septic stench as you cross Mahim Creek, where bikers park on the soaring bridge to shoot the breeze amid fumes that could drop an elephant; the feeling of diesel permeating your bloodstream and the manically reverberating mantra of 'Horn OK Please' as you ooze through traffic past Worli's glitzy shopping malls and the fairytale island mosque of Haji Ali. And finally the magic moment as you swing out on to Chowpatty Beach and the city throws off her cloak of chaos to reveal a neon-painted skyscape that makes you feel like you've arrived at the centre of all things.

Gothic clocktowers and glass skyscrapers, mill chimneys and minarets, vibrant temples and tarpaulin-roofed shacks mingle below the smog. Stitching them together are streets aswarm with panel-beaten double-decker buses, yellow and black taxis, long wooden carts stacked with hessian-stitched parcels being towed by teams of grimacing Bihari migrant workers, and white-hatted dabbawalas weaving their way through the chaos carrying stacks of metal tins – the guardians of a hundred thousand office lunches.

Ins and outs → *Phone code: 022.*

Getting there
Chhatrapati Shivaji International Airport (BOM) is 30 km north of Nariman Point, the business heart of the city. The domestic terminals at Santa Cruz are 5 km closer. Pre-paid taxis to the city centre are good value and take 40-90 minutes; buses are cheaper but significantly slower. If you arrive at night without a hotel booking it is best to stay at one of the hotels near the airports. Long-distance trains arrive and depart from several distinct stations in the centre and suburbs: **Chhatrapati Shivaji Terminus** (CST), close to the hotels of Colaba, and **Mumbai Central**, a few kilometres north, are the most convenient, while **Dadar**, **Bandra** and **Lokmanya Tilak** all involve a lengthy trip into town by taxi or local train (the latter only feasible outside rush hour). State-run MSRTC buses terminate at **Mumbai Central Bus Stand**, opposite the railway station. Private interstate buses might drop you on the road outside, but those from Pune and other parts of Maharashtra tend to stop out in the suburbs, at Dadar, Bandra, Andheri or Borivali ▸▸ *See Transport, page 56.*

Getting around
The sights are spread out and you need transport. Taxis are metered and good value. Ask for the rate card for conversions. There are frequent buses on major routes, and the two suburban railway lines are useful out of peak hours, but get horrendously crowded. Auto-rickshaws are only allowed in the suburbs north of Mahim Creek.

Tourist information
Government of India ⓘ *123 M Karve Rd, opposite Churchgate, T022-2207 4333, Mon-Sat 0830-1730 (closed 2nd Sat of month from 1230); counters open 24 hrs at both airports; Taj Mahal Hotel, Mon-Sat 0830-1530 (closed 2nd Sat from 1230).* Helpful staff who can also issue liquor permits (essential for Gujarat). **Maharashtra Tourist Development Corporation** (MTDC) ⓘ *CDO Hutments, Madam Cama Rd, T022-2204 4040, www.maharashtratourism.gov.in; Koh-i-Noor Rd, near Pritam Hotel, Dadar T022-2414 3200; CST Railway Station, T022-2262 2859.* Information and booking counters at international and domestic terminals and online.

Background

Hinduism made its mark on Mumbai long before the Portuguese and British transformed it into one of India's great cities. The caves on the island of Elephanta were excavated under the Kalachuris (AD 500-600). Yet, only 350 years ago, the area occupied by this great metropolis comprised seven islands inhabited by Koli fishermen. The British acquired these marshy and malarial islands as part of the marriage dowry paid by the Portuguese when Catherine of Braganza married Charles II in 1661. Four years later, they took possession of the remaining islands and neighbouring mainland area and in 1668 the East India Company leased the whole area from the crown for £10 a year, which was paid for nearly 50 years. The East India Company shifted its headquarters to Mumbai in 1672.

Isolated by the sharp face of the Western Ghats and the constantly hostile Marathas, Mumbai's early fortunes rested on the shipbuilding yards established by progressive Parsis. It thrived entirely on overseas trade and, in the cosmopolitan city this created,

Parsis, Sephardic Jews and the British shared common interests and responded to the same incentives.

After a devastating fire on 17 February 1803, a new town with wider streets was built. Then, with the abolition of the Company's trade monopoly, the doors to rapid expansion were flung open and Mumbai flourished. Trade with England boomed, and under the governorship of Sir Bartle Frere (1862-1869) the city acquired a number of extravagant Indo-Gothic landmarks, most notably the station formerly known as the Victoria Terminus. The opening of the Suez Canal in 1870 gave Mumbai greater proximity to European markets and a decisive advantage over its eastern rival Kolkata. It has since become the headquarters for many national and international companies, and was a natural choice as home to India's stock exchange (BSE). With the sponsorship of the Tata family, Mumbai has also become the primary home of India's nuclear research programme, with its first plutonium extraction plant at Trombay in 1961 and the establishment of the Tata Institute for Fundamental Research, the most prestigious science research institute in the country.

Mumbai is still growing fast, and heavy demand for building space means property value is some of the highest on earth. As in Manhattan, buildings are going upward: residential skyscrapers have mushroomed in the upscale enclaves around Malabar Hill. Meanwhile, the old mill complexes of Lower Parel have been rapidly revived as shopping and luxury apartment complexes. An even more ambitious attempt to ease pressure on the isthmus is the newly minted city of Navi Mumbai, 90 minutes east of the city, which has malls, apartments and industrial parks, but little of the glamour that makes Mumbai such a magnet.

The latest project is the controversial redevelopment of Dharavi, a huge chunk of prime real estate that's currently occupied by Asia's biggest slum – home to one third of Mumbai's population, in desperately squalid makeshift hovels originally designed to house migrant mill workers. In addition, an uncounted number live precariously in unauthorized, hastily rigged and frequently demolished corrugated iron or bamboo-and-tarpaulin shacks beside railways and roads, while yet more sleep in doorways and on sheets across the pavement.

In recent decades, the pressure of supporting so many people has begun to tell on Mumbai. Communal riots between Hindus and Muslims have flared up several times since the destruction by militant Hindus of the Babri Masjid in 1992, and the disastrous 2005 monsoon, which dumped almost a metre of rainfall on the city overnight and left trains stranded with water up to their windows, laid bare the governmental neglect which had allowed drainage and other infrastructure to lag behind the needs of the populace.

The unprecedented attacks of 26 November 2008, when Lashkar-e-Taiba terrorists held staff and foreign guests hostage in the Taj Mahal and Oberoi hotels, have been widely read as a strike against the symbols of India's overseas business ambitions. They further served to illustrate that money cannot buy protection from the harsh realities of Indian life. Yet the citizens did not vent their anger on each other, but at the government that had failed to deal effectively with the attacks. Within weeks the front of the Taj had been scrubbed clean and tourists were packing out the Leopold Café, while CST station emerged from the bullets a cleaner, calmer, less chaotic place. Somehow, whether through economic imperative or a shared mentality of forward thinking, the city always finds a way to bounce back.

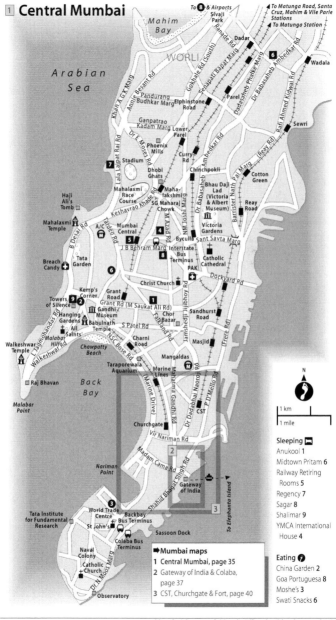

Central Mumbai

To ⑧ & Airports
Sivaji Park

To Matunga Road, Santa Cruz, Mahim & Vile Parle Stations

To Matunga Station

Mahim Bay

WORLI

Arabian Sea

Dadar

Ranade Rd

Gokhale Rd (South)

Senapati Bapat Marg

Badasaheb Phalke Marg

⑥

Wadala

Dr Babasaheb Ambedkar Rd

Khan A GK Marg

Annie Besant Rd

Pandurang Budhkar Marg

Elphinstone Road

Parel

Sewri

Dr E Moses Rd

Ganpatrao Kadam Marg

Lower Parel

Dr Babasaheb Ambedkar Rd

Rafi Ahmed Kidwai Rd

Tilak Nath Pai Marg (Reay Rd)

Phoenix Mills

Curry Rd

Chinchpokli

Cotton Green

Dr Babasaheb Ambedkar Rd

Barrister Nath Pai Marg

Stadium

⑦

Tulsi Lajpat Rai Rd

Dhobi Ghats

Maha-lakshmi

Bhau Daji Lad (Victoria & Albert Museum)

Reay Road

Haji Ali's Tomb

Mahalaxmi Race Course

SG Maharaj Chowk

NM Joshi Marg

Victoria Gardens

Mahalaxmi Temple

Keshavrao Khade Rd

A/C Rd

Mumbai Central

④

Byculla

Sant Savta Marg

Breach Candy

Tardeo Rd

⑤

Interstate Bus Terminus

Catholic Cathedral

B Desai Rd

Tata Garden

J B Behram Marg

PAK

Dockyard Rd

⑥

Christ Church

Kemp's Corner

Grant Road

Pd Knight Marg (Jyotiba Phule)

Towers of Silence

⑨②

Grant Rd (M Saukat Ali Rd)

Sandhurst Road

Hanging Gardens

Gandhi Museum

Chor Bazar

S Patel Rd

Babulnath Temple

Masjid

Walkeshwar Temple

All Saints

Charni Road

Frere Rd

Lt Dilip Gupte Rd

Malabar Hill Rd

Walkeshwar

NSC Bose Rd

Mangaldas

Dr Dadabhai Naoroji Rd

Raj Bhavan

Chowpatty Beach

Marine Lines

Ⓜ

Malabar Point

Taraporewala Aquarium

Marine Drive

Mahatma Gandhi Rd

Dr Dadabhai Naoroji Rd

Back Bay

CST

Churchgate

Vir Nariman Rd

N

Nariman Point

Madam Cama Rd

②

Shahid Bhagat Singh Rg

Gateway of India

③

To Elephanta Island

Tata Institute for Fundamental Research

World Trade Centre

③

St John's

Backbay Bus Terminus

Sassoon Dock

Naval Colony

Colaba Bus Terminus

Catholic Church

D'N Moor Marg

Observatory

1 km	
1 mile	

➡ **Mumbai maps**

1 Central Mumbai, page 35
2 Gateway of India & Colaba, page 37
3 CST, Churchgate & Fort, page 40

Sleeping 🛏

Anukool 1
Midtown Pritam 6
Railway Retiring Rooms 5
Regency 7
Sagar 8
Shalimar 9
YMCA International House 4

Eating 🍴

China Garden 2
Goa Portuguesa 8
Moshe's 3
Swati Snacks 6

Gateway of India and Colaba → *For listings, see page 45-59.*

Hundreds of fresh migrants arrive in the city daily, and whether they come by plane, sweeping in over the crescent bays and the smog-wrapped slums bound for South Mumbai, where real estate is more expensive than Manhattan, or by packed train carriage through the endless sprawl of apartment blocks to eke out a space among the poorest of the poor in Dharavi, Mumbai, somehow, finds a way to absorb them all.

The Indo-Saracenic-style Gateway of India (1927), designed by George Wittet to commemorate the visit of George V and Queen Mary in 1911, is modelled in honey-coloured basalt on 16th-century Gujarati work. The great gateway is an archway with halls on each side capable of seating 600 at important receptions. The arch was the point from which the last British regiment left on 28 February 1948, signalling the end of the empire. The whole area has a huge buzz at weekends. Scores of boats depart from here for **Elephanta Island,** creating a sea-swell which young boys delight in diving into. Hawkers, beggars and the general throng of people all add to the atmosphere. A short distance behind the Gateway is an impressive **statue of Shivaji**.

The original red-domed **Taj Mahal Hotel** was almost completely gutted by fire in the aftermath of the 26/11 terrorist attacks, which saw guests and staff of the hotel taken hostage and several killed, but the outside has been swiftly restored to normal and the adjoining **Taj Mahal Inter-Continental**, a modern skyscraper, has fully reopened for business. It is worth popping into the Taj for a bite to eat or a drink, or to go to the nightclub with its clientele of well-heeled young Indians. Unfortunately, drug addicts, drunks and prostitutes frequent the area behind the hotel, but you can also find couples and young families taking in the sea air around the Gateway at night.

South of the Gateway of India is the crowded southern section of Shahid (literally 'martyr') Bhagat Singh Marg, or Colaba Causeway, a brilliantly bawdy bazar and the epicentre of Mumbai's tourist scene; you can buy everything from high-end jeans to cheaply made *kurtas* and knock-off leather wallets at the street stalls, and the colourful cast of characters includes Bollywood casting agents, would-be novelists plotting a successor to *Shantaram* in the **Leopold Café** (another bearer of bullet scars from the November 2008 attacks), and any number of furtive hash sellers. The Afghan Memorial **Church of St John the Baptist** (1847-1858) is at the northern edge of Colaba itself. Early English in style, with a 58-m spire, it was built to commemorate the soldiers who died in the First Afghan War. Fishermen still unload their catch early in the morning at **Sassoon Dock**, the first wet dock in India; photography prohibited. Beyond the church near the tip of the Colaba promontory lie the **Observatory** and **Old European cemetery** in the naval colony (permission needed to enter). Frequent buses ply this route.

Fort

The area stretching north from Colaba to CST (Victoria Terminus) is named after Fort St George, built by the British East India Company in the 1670s and torn down by Governor Bartle Frere in the 1860s. Anchored by the superb Chhatrapati Shivaji Museum to the south and the grassy parkland of Oval Maidan to the west, this area blossomed after 1862, when Sir Bartle Frere became governor (1862-1867). Under his enthusiastic guidance

Mumbai became a great civic centre and an extravaganza of Victorian Gothic architecture, modified by Indo-Saracenic influences. This area is worth exploring at night, when many of the old buildings are floodlit.

2 Gateway of India & Colaba

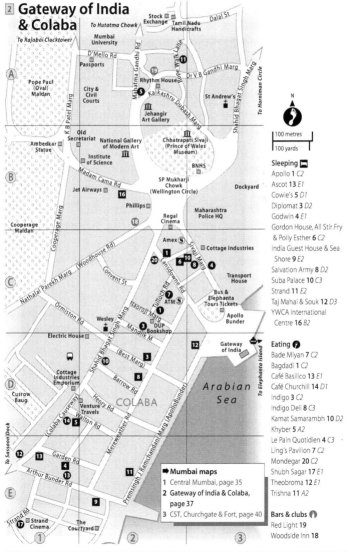

Sleeping
Apollo **1** *C2*
Ascot **13** *E1*
Cowie's **5** *D1*
Diplomat **3** *D2*
Godwin **4** *E1*
Gordon House, All Stir.Fry & Polly Esther **6** *C2*
India Guest House & Sea Shore **9** *E2*
Salvation Army **8** *D2*
Suba Palace **10** *C3*
Strand **11** *E2*
Taj Mahal & Souk **12** *D3*
YWCA International Centre **16** *B2*

Eating
Bade Miyan **7** *C2*
Bagdadi **1** *C2*
Café Basilico **13** *E1*
Café Churchill **14** *D1*
Indigo **3** *C3*
Indigo Deli **8** *C3*
Kamat Samarambh **10** *D2*
Khyber **5** *A2*
Le Pain Quotidien **4** *C3*
Ling's Pavilion **7** *C2*
Mondegar **20** *C2*
Shubh Sagar **17** *E1*
Theobroma **12** *E1*
Trishna **11** *A2*

Bars & clubs
Red Light **19**
Woodside Inn **18**

➡ **Mumbai maps**

Chhatrapati Shivaji (Prince of Wales) Museum ① *Oct-Feb Tue-Sun 1015-1800, last tickets 1645; foreigners Rs 300 (includes audio guide), Indians Rs 15, camera Rs 15 (no flash or tripods), students Rs 10, children Rs 5, avoid Tue as it is busy with school visits,* is housed in an impressive building designed by George Wittet to commemorate the visit of the Prince of Wales to India in 1905. The dome of glazed tiles has a very Persian and Central Asian flavour. The archaeological section has three main groups: Brahminical; Buddhist and Jain; Prehistoric and Foreign. The art section includes an excellent collection of Indian miniatures and well displayed *tankhas* along with a section on armour that is worth seeing. There are also works by Gainsborough, Poussin and Titian as well as Indian silver, jade and tapestries. The Natural History section is based on the collection of the Bombay Natural History Society, founded in 1833. Good guidebooks, cards and reproductions are on sale. **Jehangir Art Gallery** ① *within the museum complex, T022-2284 3989,* holds short-term exhibitions of contemporary art. The **Samovar café** is good for a snack and a chilled beer in a pleasant, if cramped, garden-side setting. Temporary members may use the library and attend lectures.

The **National Gallery of Modern Art** ① *Sir Cowasji Jehangir Hall, opposite the museum, T022-2285 2457, foreigners Rs 150, Indians Rs 10,* is a three-tiered gallery converted from an old public hall which gives a good introduction to India's contemporary art scene.

St Andrew's Kirk (1819) ① *just behind the museum, daily 1000-1700,* is a simple neoclassical church. At the south end of Mahatma Gandhi (MG) Road is the renaissance-style **Institute of Science** (1911) designed by George Wittet. The institute, which includes a scientific library, a public hall and examination halls, was built with gifts from the Parsi and Jewish communities.

The **Oval Maidan** has been restored to a pleasant public garden and acts as the lungs and public cricket pitch of the southern business district. On the east side of the **Pope Paul Maidan** is the Venetian Gothic-style **old Secretariat** (1874), with a façade of arcaded verandas and porticos that are faced in buff-coloured Porbander stone from Gujarat. Decorated with red and blue basalt, the carvings are in white *hemnagar* stone. The **University Convocation Hall** (1874) to its north was designed by Sir George Gilbert Scott in a 15th-century French decorated style. Scott also designed the adjacent **University Library** and the **Rajabai clock tower** (1870s) next door, based on Giotto's campanile in Florence. The sculpted figures in niches on the exterior walls of the tower were designed to represent the castes of India. Originally the clock could chime 12 tunes including *Rule Britannia*. The **High Court** (1871-1879), in early English Gothic style, has a 57-m-high central tower flanked by lower octagonal towers topped by the figures of Justice and Mercy. The Venetian Gothic **Public Works Office** (1869-1872) is to its north. Opposite, and with its main façade to Vir Nariman Road, is the gorgeously wrought former **General Post Office** (1869-1872). Now called the Telegraph Office, it stands next to the original Telegraph Office adding romanesque to the extraordinary mixture of European architectural styles.

From here you can walk east and delve into the dense back lanes of the Fort district, crossing the five-way junction of **Hutatma Chowk** ('Martyrs' Corner', in the centre of which stands the architecturally forgettable but useful landmark of the Flora Fountain (1869). This is an interesting area to explore although there are no particular sights

Vir Nariman Road cuts through to the elegant tree-shaded oval of **Horniman Circle** , laid out in 1860 and renamed in 1947 after Benjamin Horniman, editor of the pro-independence *Bombay Chronicle* – one of the few English names remaining on the Mumbai map. The park in the middle is used for dance and music performances during the **Kala Ghoda Arts Festival**, held in January. On the west edge are the Venetian Gothic **Elphinstone Buildings** (1870) in brown sandstone, while to the south is the **Cathedral Church of St Thomas** (1718), which contains a number of monuments amounting to a heroic 'Who's Who of India'.

South of Horniman Circle on Shahid Bhagat Singh Marg, the **Custom House** is one of the oldest buildings in the city, believed to incorporate a Portuguese barrack block from 1665. Over the entrance is the crest of the East India Company. Remnants of the old Portuguese fort's walls can be seen and many Malabar teak 'East Indiamen' ships were built here. Walk north from here and you'll reach the **Town Hall** (1820-1823), widely admired and much photographed as one of the best neoclassical buildings in India. The Corinthian interior houses the **Assembly Rooms** and the **Bombay Asiatic Society**. Immediately north again is the **Mint** (1824-1829) ① *visit by prior permission from the Mint Master, T022-2270 3184, www.mumbaimint.org*, built on the Fort rubbish dump, with Ionic columns and a water tank in front of it. The nearby **Ballard Estate** is also worth a poke around while you're in the area, with some good hotels and restaurants, as well as Hamilton Studios, the swanky offices of *Vogue* magazine, and the Mumbai Port Authority.

Around the CST (VT)

Chhatrapati Shivaji Terminus (1878-1887), formerly Victoria Terminus and still known to many elder taxi drivers as 'VT', is far and away the most remarkable example of Victorian Gothic architecture in India. Opened during Queen Victoria's Golden Jubilee year (1887), over three million commuters now swarm through the station daily, though the bustling chaos of old has been reined in somewhat since November 2008's terror attacks, when at least 50 people were shot dead here. Several scenes from *Slumdog Millionaire* were filmed on the suburban platforms at the west end of the station.

The station was built at a time when fierce debate was taking place among British architects working in India as to the most appropriate style to develop to meet the demands of the late 19th-century boom. One view held that the British should restrict themselves to models derived from the best in Western tradition. Others argued that architects should draw on Indian models, trying to bring out the best of Indian tradition and encourage its development. By and large, the former were dominant, but the introduction of Gothic elements allowed a blending of Western traditions with Indian (largely Islamic) motifs, which became known as the Indo-Saracenic style. The station that resulted, designed by FW Stevens, is its crowning glory: a huge, symmetrical, gargoyle-studded frontage capped by a large central dome and a 4-m-high statue of Progress, with arcaded booking halls, stained glass and glazed tiles inspired by St Pancras. The giant caterpillar-like walkway with perspex awnings looks truly incongruous against the huge Gothic structure.

There are many more Victorian buildings in the area around CST, particularly along Mahapalika Marg (Cruickshank Road), which runs northwest of the station past the grand **Municipal Buildings** (also by Stevens, 1893), and Lokmanya Tilak Marg (Camac Road), which joins Mahapalika Marg at the Metro Cinema traffic circle – a landmark known to every Mumbai cabbie.

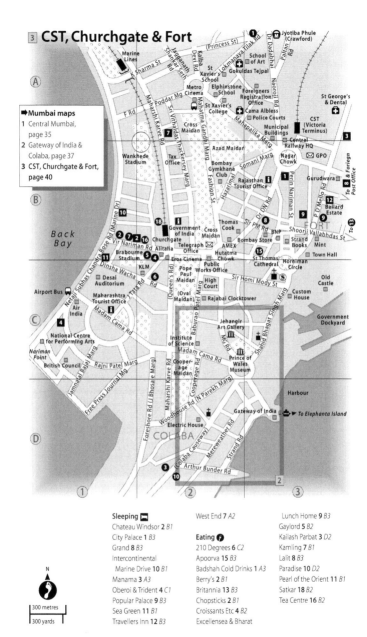

3 CST, Churchgate & Fort

➡ **Mumbai maps**
1 Central Mumbai, page 35
2 Gateway of India & Colaba, page 37
3 CST, Churchgate & Fort, page 40

Sleeping 🛏
Chateau Windsor **2** B1
City Palace **1** B3
Grand **8** B3
Intercontinental Marine Drive **10** B1
Manama **3** A3
Oberoi & Trident **4** C1
Popular Palace **9** B3
Sea Green **11** B1
Travellers Inn **12** B3
West End **7** A2

Eating 🍴
210 Degrees **6** C2
Apoorva **15** B3
Badshah Cold Drinks **1** A3
Berry's **2** B1
Britannia **13** B3
Chopsticks **2** B1
Croissants Etc **4** B2
Excellensea & Bharat

Lunch Home **9** B3
Gaylord **5** B2
Kailash Parbat **3** D2
Kamling **7** B1
Lalit **8** B3
Paradise **10** D2
Pearl of the Orient **11** B1
Satkar **18** B2
Tea Centre **16** B2

Immediately to the north of CST lies **Crawford Market** (1865-1871), now renamed **Mahatma Jyotiba Phule Market** after a Maharashtran social reformer, designed by Emerson in 12th-century French Gothic style, with paving stones imported from Caithness and fountains carved by Lockwood Kipling. The market is divided into bustling sections for fruit, vegetables, fish, mutton and poultry, with a large central hall and clock tower.

Running northwest of Crawford Market towards Mumbai Central Railway Station is **Falkland Road**, the centre of Mumbai's red-light district. Prostitutes stand behind barred windows, giving the area its other name, 'The Cages' – many of the girls are sold or abducted from various parts of India and Nepal. AIDS is very widespread, and a lot of NGOs are at work in the area educating the women about prevention.

North of Crawford Market is **Masjid Station**, the heart of the Muslim quarter, where agate minarets mingle with the pollution-streaked upper storeys of 1960s residential towers. The atmosphere here is totally different from the crumbling colonial architectural glory of the Colaba and Fort area: balconies on faded apartment blocks are bedecked with fairy lights, laundry dries on the window grilles, and at sunset the ramshackle roads hum with taxis, boys wielding wooden carts through traffic and Muslim women at a stroll. One of the city's most interesting markets, the **Chor Bazar** (Thieves' Market) ① *Sat to Thu 1100-1900*, spreads through the streets between the station and Falkland Road. The bazar is a great place to poke around in with tonnes of dealers in old watches, film posters, Belgian- or Indian-made temple lamps, enamel tiles and door knobs. The area around Mutton Street is popular with film prop-buyers and foreign and domestic bric-a-brac hunters.

Marine Drive to Malabar Hill

When the hustle of the city becomes too much, do as the Mumbaikars do and head for the water. The 3-km sweep of **Marine Drive** (known as the 'Queen's Necklace' for the lines of streetlights that run its length) skirts alongside the grey waters of the Arabian Sea from Nariman Point in the south to exclusive Malabar Hill in the north. This is where you'll see Mumbai at its most egalitarian: servants and *babus* alike take the air on the esplanades in the evening. For an interesting half-day trip, start downtown at Churchgate Station and follow the curving course of the Queen's Necklace to the Walkeshwar Temple out on the end of Malabar Hill; start at lunchtime and you can be strolling back down Marine Drive, ice cream in hand, among the atmospheric sunset crush of power-walking executives and festive families.

Churchgate Station (1894-1896), on Vir Nariman Road at the north end of the Oval Maidan, was the second great railway building designed by FW Stevens. With its domes and gables, Churchgate has an air of Byzantine simplicity that contrasts with CST's full-tilt Gothic overload, but the rush hour spectacle is no less striking: Sebastiao Salgado's famous photograph of commuters pouring out of suburban trains was taken here.

A block to the west is Netaji Subhash Road, better known as **Marine Drive**, which bends northwest past Wankhede cricket stadium, several luxury hotels and the run-down Taraporewala Aquarium. At the north end in the crook of Malabar Hill is **Chowpatty Beach**, a long stretch of grey-white sand that looks attractive from a distance, but is polluted. Swimming here is not recommended but there is a lot of interesting beach activity in the evening. Chowpatty was the scene of a number of important 'Quit India' rallies during the Independence Movement. During important festivals, like **Ganesh Chaturthi** and **Dussehra** (see Festivals and events, page 52), it is thronged with jubilant Hindu devotees.

Mahatma Gandhi Museum (**Mani Bhavan**) ① *west of Grant Rd station at 19 Laburnum Rd, www.gandhi-manibhavan.org, 0930-1800, Rs 10, allow 1 hr*, is north of Chowpatty on the road to Nana Chowk. This private house, where Mahatma Gandhi used to stay on visits to Mumbai, is now a memorial museum and research library with 20,000 volumes. There is a diorama depicting important scenes from Gandhi's life, but the display of photos and letters on the first floor is more interesting, and includes letters Gandhi wrote to Hitler in 1939 asking him not to go to war, and those to Roosevelt, Einstein and Tolstoy.

At the end of Chowpatty, Marine Drive becomes Walkeshwar Road and bends southwest to pass the **Jain Temple** (1904), built of marble and dedicated to the first Jain Tirthankar. Much of the colourful decoration depicts the lives of the Tirthankars. Visitors can watch various rituals being performed. Jains play a prominent part in Mumbai's banking and commerce and are one of the city's wealthiest communities. Beyond, on the tip of Malabar Point, is **Raj Bhavan**, now home to the Governor of Maharashtra.

Behind the Jain Temple, Gangadhar Kher Rd (Ridge Road) runs up Malabar Hill to the **Hanging Gardens** (**Pherozeshah Mehta Gardens**) so named since they are located on top of a series of tanks that supply water to Mumbai. The gardens are well kept with lots of topiary animals and offer an opportunity to hang out with Mumbai's elite, whose penthouse apartments peer down on the park from all sides; there are good views over the city and Marine Drive from the **Kamala Nehru Park** across the road. It's worth a visit after 1700 when it's a bit cooler, but it's reputed to be unsafe after nightfall. Immediately to the north are the Parsi **Towers of Silence**, set in secluded gardens donated by Parsi industrialist Sir Jamshetji Jeejeebhoy. This very private place is not accessible to tourists but it can be glimpsed from the road. Parsis believe that the elements of water, fire and earth must not be polluted by the dead, so they lay their 'vestments of flesh and bone' out on the top of the towers to be picked clean by vultures. The depletion in the number of vultures is a cause for concern, and more and more agiarys now opt for solar panels to speed up the process of decay.

At the end of the headland behind Raj Bhavan stands the **Walkeshwar Temple** ('Lord of Sand'), built about AD 1000 and one of the oldest buildings in Mumbai. In legend this was a resting point for Lord Rama on his journey from Ayodhya to Lanka to free Sita from the demon king Ravana. One day Rama's brother failed to return from Varanasi at the usual time with a *lingam* that he fetched daily for Rama's worship. Rama then made a *lingam* from the beach sand to worship Siva. You'd also do well to visit **Banganga**, a freshwater tank that's part of an 12th-century temple complex. Legend has it that when Rama got thirsty Lakshman raised his bow and shot a *baan* (arrow) into the ground, bringing forth fresh water from the Ganga in this ocean locked island. The site is being renovated and is regularly used as a venue for concerts, festivals and pilgrimages alike.

Dabbawallahs

If you go inside Churchgate station at mid-morning or after lunch, you will see the *dabbawallahs*, members of the Bombay Union of Tiffin Box Carriers. Each morning, the 2500 *dabbawallahs* call on suburban housewives who pack freshly cooked lunch into small circular stainless steel containers – *dabbas*. Three or four are stacked one on the other and held together by a clip with a handle. Typically the *dabbawallah* will collect 30-40 tiffin boxes, range them out on a long pole and cycle to the nearest station. Here he will hand them over to a fellow *dabbawallah* who will transport them into the city for delivery.

Over 100,000 lunches of maybe *sabze* (vegetable curry), chappattis, dahl and pickle make their way daily across town to the breadwinner. The service, which costs a few rupees a day, is a good example of the fine division of labour in India, reliable and efficient, for the *dabbawallahs* pride themselves on never losing a lunch. He makes sure that the carefully prepared *pukka* (proper) food has not in any way been defiled.

Central Mumbai

Other than to catch a train from Mumbai Central Station, relatively few visitors venture into the area north of Marine Drive, yet it contains some fascinating only-in-Mumbai sights which, with judicious use of taxis and the odd suburban train, can easily be combined into a day trip with the coastal sights described above.

On the coast, 1 km north of the Ghandi Museum on Bhulabhai Desai (Warden Road), is the **Mahalakshmi Temple**, the oldest in Mumbai, dedicated to three goddesses whose images were found in the sea. Lakshmi, goddess of wealth, is the unofficial presiding deity of the city, and the temple is host to frenzied activity – pressing a coin into the wall of the main shrine is supposed to be a sign of riches to come. Just to the north, **Haji Ali's Mosque** sits on an islet 500 m offshore. The mosque, built in 1431, contains the tomb of Muslim saint Haji Ali, who drowned here while on pilgrimage to Mecca, and as a last request demanded that he be buried neither on land nor at sea. A long causeway, usable only at low tide, links the mosque and tomb to the land, and is lined by Muslim supplicants. The money changers are willing to exchange one-rupee coins into smaller coins, enabling pilgrims to make several individual gifts to beggars rather than one larger one, thereby reputedly increasing the merit of the gift.

From Haji Ali's Tomb go east along Keshavrao Khade Road, passing the **Mahalakshmi Race Course** ① *racing season Nov-Apr, www.rwitc.com*, to SG Maharaj Chowk (**Jacob's Circle**), and turn north to Mahalakshmi Bridge, reachable by local trains from Churchgate. From the bridge there is a view across the astonishing Municipal **dhobi ghats**, where Mumbai's dirty laundry is soaked, smacked in concrete tubs and aired in public by the *dhobis* (washerfolk); vistas unfold in blocks of primary colours, though you may have to fend off junior touts to enjoy them in peace. A short distance further north are the disused Victorian cotton mills of **Lower Parel**. Closed in 1980 after an all-out strike, some remain standing in a state of picturesque ruin (local residents may offer to show you round for Rs 50-100) while others, notably the Phoenix, Mathuradas and Bombay Dyeing mill compounds, have been converted into slick new malls, nightclubs and studio spaces popular with publishers and advertising agencies.

Southeast of Mahalakshmi station in Byculla are the **Veermata Jijibai Bhonsle Udyan** gardens, formerly Victoria Gardens. The attractive 20-ha park is home to Mumbai's **zoo** ① *Thu-Tue 0900-1800, Rs 5*, be warned though, the signboards are missing and while the birds are gorgeous – they have birds of paradise, white peacocks and pink pelicans among others – there's no indication of what you're looking at. The gardens share space with the newly renovated **Bhau Daji Lad Museum** (**Victoria and Albert Museum**) ① *www.bdlmuseum.org, Thu-Tue 1000-1730, foreigners Rs 100, Indians Rs 10, children half price*. Inspired by the V&A in London and financed by public subscription, it was built in 1872 in a palladian style and is the second oldest museum in India. The collection covers the history of Mumbai and contains prints, maps and models that show how the seven disjointed islands came to form Mumbai.

Bandra, Juhu Beach and Andheri

If you really want to get under the skin of the city, a jaunt into the far-flung northern suburbs is essential. Close to the airports and relatively relaxed compared to living in the city centre, Bandra and Juhu are popular with Mumbai's upper crust, and most Bollywood A-listers have at least one of their homes here. **Bandra** is a lively suburb, full of the young and wealthy, with some exciting places to eat and some of the coolest bars, coffee shops, gyms and lounges in the city. Linking Road is home to a long open-air shoe bazar where you can find cheap, colourful sandals and knock-offs of every brand of clothing. Bandra's two seaside promenades, one at Bandra Bandstand by the **Taj Lands End Hotel** and one at Carter Road, the next bay northwards, feature sea-facing coffee shops with spectacular sunset views.

Juhu Beach, 20 km north of the centre, used to be an attractive and relaxed seaside area, but one sniff of the toxic water oozing out of Mahim Creek is enough to dissuade anyone from dipping so much as a toe in the ocean. Hordes of people still visit every day to walk on the beach, eat *bhel puri* and other spicy street food that delicate stomachs had best avoid, while kids buy balloons and take rides on horse-driven chariots. Beyond the beach Juhu is primarily a residential area, full of luxurious apartments, elegant old bungalows (Bollywood megastar Amitabh Bachchan has a place here) and day spas.

Andheri, spreading north of the airports, is the biggest suburb in Mumbai: it covers 50 sq km, is home to between 1.5 million and four million people depending on who's counting, and has sprung up from villages and mangrove swamps in a mere 30 years. There are few sights of note, but as a city within a city, with its own social subdivisions (mega-trendy residential enclaves and malls to the west, business parks and down-at-heel slums to the east, and even a suburban monorail system in construction), Andheri may well come to represent Mumbai's second city centre. If you want to explore, the areas to know about are Lokhandwala, New Link Road and Seven Bungalows/Versova; all are in Andheri West.

Mumbai (Bombay) listings

Hotel prices

$$$$	over US$1500	**$$$**	US$66-1500
$$	US$30-65	**$**	under US$30

Restaurant prices

$$$	over US$12	**$$**	US$6-12
$	under US$6		

⊙ Sleeping

Room prices in Mumbai are stratospheric by Indian standards, and there's no such thing as low-season: if possible make reservations in advance or arrive as early in the day as you can. Most hotels are concentrated in the downtown area, between **Colaba** and **Marine Dr**, and around the airport in the suburbs of **Santa Cruz**, **Juhu**, **Bandra** and **Andheri**. There are also several options around Mumbai Central and Dadar stations – handy for a quick getaway or an un-touristy view of the city.

Backpackers usually head for the **Colaba** area, which has the only acceptable cheap rooms in the city. **Arthur Bunder Rd** is a hotspot, with several places hidden away on upper floors of apartment blocks, usually with shared facilities, cold water and windowless rooms; arrive early and inspect room first. For guest accommodation contact **India Tourism**, 123 M Karve Rd, Churchgate, T022-2203 3144. You can also look on www.ndtvclassifieds.com.

Gateway of India and Colaba *p36, map p37*

Rooms with a sea view are more expensive. There are few budget hotels left in the area charging under Rs 800, though you can still find a dormitory bed for Rs 200.

$$$$ Ascot, 38 Garden Rd, T022-6638 5566, www.ascothotel.com. The tan-wood rooms, shoehorned into a graceful 1930s building, veer dangerously close to IKEA anonymity, but they're generously proportioned and new, with safe deposit boxes, work desks and granite shower stalls. Great views from the upper floors. Breakfast included.

$$$$ Gordon House Hotel, 5 Battery St, Apollo Bunder, Colaba, T022-2289 4400, www.ghhotel.com. A spruce boutique hotel in the edgy Colaba district. 3 themed floors that really do leave India outside: yellow Med-style walls, quilts in the country cottage rooms and blonde wood on the Scandinavian floor.

$$$$ Taj Mahal, Apollo Bunder, T022-6665 3366, www.tajhotels.com. The grand dame of Mumbai lodging, over a century old. The glorious old wing has been fully restored and updated after the 26/11/08 attacks, joining the 306 rooms in the **Taj Mahal Intercontinental** tower. Several top-class restaurants and bars, plus fitness centre, superb pool and even a yacht on call.

$$$ Apollo, 22 Lansdowne Rd, Colaba, behind **Taj**, T022-2287 3312, hotelapollogh@ hotmail.com. 39 rooms, some a/c, some amazing sea views. Tatty linen and walls, but friendly staff.

$$$ Diplomat, 24-26 BK Boman Behram Marg, behind **Taj**, T022-2202 1661, www.hoteldiplomat-bombay.com. 52 a/c rooms, restaurant, quiet, friendly, relaxed atmosphere, good value. Very simple furnishings, small beds. Recommended.

$$$ Godwin, 41 Garden Rd, T022-2287 2050, www.hotelgodwin.co.in. 48 large, clean, renovated, a/c rooms with superb views from upper floors, mostly helpful management and a good rooftop restaurant – full of wealthy Mumbaikars on Fri and Sat night.

$$$ Strand, 25 PJ Ramchandani Marg, T022-2288 2222, www.hotelstrand.com. Friendly. Clean rooms, some with bath and sea view.

$$$ Suba Palace, Apollo Bunder, T022-2220 2063, www.hotelsubapalace.com. Clean, modern, well run. Recommended.

$$$ YWCA International Centre, 2nd floor, 18 Madam Cama Rd, T022-2202 0598, www.ywcaic.info. For both sexes, 34 clean, pleasant rooms with bath, breakfast and dinner included, essential to write in advance with Rs 1300 deposit. Recommended.

$$ Cowie's, 15 Walton Rd, near Electric House, Colaba T022-2284 0232. 20 rooms with central a/c, bathroom en suite, TV and phone, in old-world hotel on one of the tree-lined residential streets off Colaba Causeway. Excellent value.

$ India Guest House, 1/49 Kamal Mansion, Arthur Bunder Rd, T022-2283 3769. 20 rooms along long corridor, white partitions that you could, at a push, jump over. Fan, no toilet or shower. The corner room has a neat panorama over the bay. Sound will travel.

$ The Salvation Army, Red Shield House, 30 Mereweather Rd, T022-2284 1824, redshield@vsnl.net. The only remotely backpacker-orientated place in Mumbai, with dorms (Rs 200 including breakfast) and some doubles and triples, a few with a/c. Rooms have high ceilings and there's a sociable canteen, but the internet is slow, shared bathrooms are dilapidated, and the mattresses can be something of a bedbug fest. Checkout 0900, lockers obligatory for dorm guests. Book in advance or arrive early.

$ Sea Shore, top floor, 1/49 Kamal Mansion, Arthur Bunder Rd, T022-2287 4238. Kitsch as you like, 15 bright gloss-pink rooms and purple corridors with plastic flowers, shower in room but no sink, 7 with window and TV and fan, 8 without. Sea view room has 4 beds. 2 rooms come with toilet, TV and hot water.

Fort *p36, map p40*

$$$ Grand, 17 Sprott Rd, Ballard Estate, T022-6658 0500, www.grandhotelbombay. com. Old-fashioned, built around a central courtyard, 73 a/c rooms, exchange, book counter, helpful service, very relaxing.

$$-$ Traveller's Inn, 26 Adi Murzban Path, Ballard Estate, T022-2264 4685, www.hoteltravellersinn.co.in. A relatively new addition to Mumbai's backpacker repertoire,

with simple, clean rooms, a 3-bed dormitory, internet and Wi-Fi, and friendly staff.

$ Popular Palace, 104-106 Mint Rd, near GPO, Fort Market, T022-2269 5506. Small but clean rooms with bath (hot water), some a/c, helpful staff, good value.

Around the CST (VT) *p39, map p40*

$$ City Palace, 121 City Terrace (Nagar Chowk), opposite CST Main Gate, T022-2261 5515. Tiny though clean, functional rooms (some no windows), with bath (Indian WC), some a/c, helpful staff, convenient location.

$$ Manama, 221 P D'Mello Rd, T022-2261 3412. Decent rooms, some with bath and a/c.

Marine Drive to Malabar Hill *p41, maps p35 and p40*

$$$$ Intercontinental Marine Drive, 135 Marine Dr, T022-3987 9999, www.mumbai.intercontinental.com. 59 rooms in luxury hotel overlooking Marine Drive. Bose stereo, plasma TV screens, Bulgari toiletries, personal butler service and beautiful rooftop pool.

$$$$ The Oberoi, Nariman Pt, T022-6632 5757, www.oberoimumbai.com. Newly renovated and reopened, with beautiful sea-view rooms, glass-walled bathrooms, and 3 top-class restaurants.

$$$$ Trident, Nariman Pt, T022-6632 4343, www.tridenthotels.com. Attached to the **Oberoi**, this 550-room tower is worth splashing out on if you can snag one of the renovated sea-view rooms on the upper floors. Good pool, spa and gym, great restaurant, but beefed-up security can make check-in slow.

$$$ Chateau Windsor Guest House, 86 Vir Nariman Rd, T022-6622 4455, www.cwh.in. Friendly and helpful place in a great location. The rooms on the 1st and 3rd floors are the best, newly renovated with large spotless bathrooms, marble tiles and balconies. Some of the older rooms are small, poky and dark. Recommended.

$$$ Shalimar, August Kranti Marg, Kemps Corner (at east end of Malabar Hill), T022-6664 1000, www.shalimarhotel.com. 80 small, pleasant suites, good restaurant but plays the same 1980s music on repeat, efficient front desk, well located, Wi-Fi.

$$$ West End, 45 New Marine Lines, T022-4083 9121, www.westendhotelmumbai.com. 80 small, pleasant suites but in need of refurbishment. Good restaurant, excellent service, efficient front desk, well located, good value. Recommended.

$$ Sea Green, 145 Marine Dr, T022-2282 2294, www.seagreenhotel.com. 34 rooms, 22 a/c, pleasant breezy informal sitting area.

Central Mumbai *p43, map p35*

$$$$-$$$ Regency, Worli, T022-6657 1234, www.regencymumbai.com. 80 clean rooms, internet, good location, personable, friendly staff, some sea-facing rooms. Good value. Recommended.

$$$ Bawa Regency, Gokuldas Pasta Rd, Dadar East, T022-4049 8383. Some a/c in the 31 rooms, mostly shared but clean baths. Flexible checkout, friendly. Recommended.

$$ Sagar, Nagpada Junction (Bellasin Rd/JB Behram Marg corner), Byculla, T022-2308 1441. Very clean rooms, good restaurant, friendly.

$$ YMCA International House, 18 YMCA Rd, near Mumbai Central, T022-6154 0100. Decent rooms, shared bath, meals included, temp membership Rs 120, deposit Rs 1300, good value, book 3 months ahead.

$ Anukool, 292-8 Maulana Saukat Ali Rd, T022-2308 0201, hotelanukool@hotmail.com. 23 rooms, some a/c, friendly, helpful, good value, but inspect room first.

Bandra, Juhu Beach and Andheri *p44*

Most hotels near the airport offer free transfer. Tourist information at the airport can book.

$$$$ Citizen, 960 Juhu Tara Rd, T022-6693 2525, www.citizenhotelmumbai.com. Despite unexciting appearance, 45 small

but very well-appointed rooms, suites, efficient airport transfer.

$$$$ Leela, near International Terminal, T022-6000 2233, www.theleela.com. 460 modern rooms, excellent restaurants, pricey but excellent bar (residents only after 2300), all-night coffee shop, happening night club.

$$$$ Novotel (formerly Holiday Inn), Balraj Sahani Marg, Juhu Beach, T022-6693 4444. Brand new, featuring 203 rooms, 1 lounge, 4 restaurants, health club and swimming pool.

$$$$ Orchid, 70C Nehru Rd, Vile Parle (east), 5 mins' walk from domestic terminal, T022- 2616 4040, www.orchidhotel.com. Refurbished, attractive rooms, eco-friendly. Boulevard restaurant boasts a good midnight buffet and '15-min lightning' buffet. Recommended.

$$$$ Sun-n-Sand, 39 Juhu Beach, T022-6693 8888, www.sunnsandhotel.com. 118 rooms, best refurbished, comfortable, though cramped poolside, good restaurant.

$$$$-$$$ Metro Palace, 355 Ramdas Nayak Rd (Hill Rd), near Bandra station (W), T022-2642 7311. Convenient, close to domestic airport and shops, good restaurant.

$$$ Juhu Plaza, 39/2 Juhu Beach, T022-6695 9600, www.hoteljuhuplaza.com. 40 rooms, excellent restaurant. Recommended.

$$$ Juhu Residency, 148B Juhu Tara Rd, T022-6783 4949, www.juhuresidency.com. Across the road from the Marriott, with just 28 attractive refurbished rooms, free Wi-Fi, friendly efficient staff and 2 excellent restaurants. A great deal by Mumbai standards.

$$$ Pali Hills, 14 Union Park, Pali Hill, Bandra, T022-2649 2995. Quiet location, near market, continental restaurant.

$$$ Residency, Suren Rd, T022-2692 3000, www.residencymumbai.com. New hotel 3 km from the airport, request free pick-up. 72 a/c smallish rooms, good restaurant, quiet back street, friendly staff. Recommended.

$$$ Transit, off Nehru Rd, Vile Parle (east), T022-6693 0761, www.hoteltransit.in. Modern, 54 rooms, reasonable overnight halt for airport,

excellent restaurant (draught beer), airport transfer. Special rates for day use (0800-1800).
$$ Atithi, 77A Nehru Rd, 7 mins' walk from domestic terminal, T022-2618 7941, www.atithihotel.net. 47 rooms, functional, clean, 3 star, set meals included, good value, efficient desk, popular.

🍴 Eating

Gateway of India and Colaba *p36, maps p35, p37 and p40*
Most restaurants in the area, including the cheaper ones, provide filtered drinking water.
$$$ All Stir Fry, Gordon House Hotel, T022-2287 1122. Oriental nosh served up in **Wagamama**-style at long shared benches. DIY food too. Don't experiment too much with the drinks though, stick to standards.
$$$ Indigo, 4 Mandlik Rd, behind **Taj Hotel**, T022-2218 2829. Excellent Mediterranean in smart restaurant, good atmosphere, additional seating on rooftop.
$$$ Indigo Deli, Chhatrapati Shivaji Maharaj Marg, T022-5655 1010. Café and deli with fresh cold cuts, sandwiches and burgers. Other meals are pricey for the quantity and quality.
$$$ Le Pain Quotidien, Dhanraj Mahal, CSM Rd, T022-6615 0202. Belgian bakery chain serving some of Mumbai's best breads and pastries, as well as light meals, salads and delectably crumbly apple pie.
$$$ Ling's Pavilion, 19/21 KC College Hostel Building, off Colaba Causeway (behind **Taj** and Regal Cinema), T022-2285 0023. Stylish decor, good atmosphere and delightful service, colourful menu, seafood specials, generous helpings.
$$$ Souk, Taj Mahal Apollo Bunder, T022-6665 3366, www.tajhotels.com. Taj's top floor is home to a North African themed restaurant. Open from 1900, great views. A glass of imported red wine (excellent though it may be) costs Rs 900 before tax.
$$ Café Basilico, Sentinel House, Arthur Bunder Rd, T022-6634 5670. Bistro with all-day breakfast and a decent Sun brunch.

Excellent *rawas*, sandwiches, desserts and coffee, but no alcohol.
$$ Moshe's, 7 Minoo Manor, next to Euphoria Gym, Bhadwar Park, Cuffe Parade, T022-2216 1226. Cosy bistro-café with great risottos and Turkish chicken. Save room for dessert.
$ Bade Miyan, Tullock Rd behind Ling's Pavilion. Streetside kebab corner, but very clean. Try *baida roti*, *shammi* and *boti* kebabs. The potato *kathi* rolls are excellent veg options.
$ Bagdadi, Tullock Rd (behind **Taj Hotel**). One of the cheapest, with first-class food, fragrant biryani, delicious chicken, crowded and utterly basic but clean. Recommended.
$ Café Churchill, 103-8, East West Court Building, opposite Cusrow Baug, Colaba Causeway, T022-2284 4689, 1000-2330. A tiny little café with 7 tables crammed with people basking in a/c, towered over by a cake counter and a Winston Churchill portrait. Great breakfasts, club sandwiches, seafood, fish and chips, lasagne and Irish stew.
$ Kamat Samarambh, opposite Electric House, Colaba Causeway. Very good and authentic South Indian food, *thalis* and snacks. Try the moist, fluffy *uttapam* and *upma*. Clean drinking water.
$ Paradise, Sindh Chambers, Colaba Causeway. Tue-Sun. Spotless Parsi place, serving excellent dhansak; try *sali boti* (mutton and 'chips').
$ Shubh Sagar, mouth of Colaba Market, Mistry Chambers, opposite Telephone Bhawan, Colaba, T022-2281 1550. 0900-2400. Excellent hygienic and clean vegetarian restaurant, great biryanis and South Indian snacks outside normal restaurant mealtimes.

Cafés and snacks
Many serve chilled beer and waiters care too much for large tips from tourist groups:
Kailash Parbat, 1st Pasta La, Colaba. Excellent snacks and chats, in an old-style eatery also serving Punjabi *thalis*. The tooth-rotting *pedas* from the counter are a Mumbai institution.

Leopold's, Colaba, T022-2283 0585. An institution among Colaba backpackers and Mumbai shoppers. The food, predominantly Western with a limited choice of Indian vegetarian, is average and pricey (similar cafés nearby are far better value) but Leo's gained cachet from its cameo role in the novel *Shantaram*, and was the first target of the terror attacks in Nov 2008.

Mondegar, near Regal Cinema. Similar to **Leopold** in spirit, but a little cheaper on the pitchers, and with a loud rock soundtrack.

Theobroma, Colaba Causeway, next to Cusrow Baug. Decent coffee and terrific egg breakfasts. The brownies here are to die for – try the millionaire brownie or the rum-and-raisin with coffee. Egg-free cakes available.

Fort *p36, maps p37 and p40*
$$$ Khyber, 145 MG Rd, Kala Ghoda, T022-2267 3227. North Indian. For an enjoyable evening in beautiful surroundings, outstanding food, especially lobster and *reshmi* chicken kebabs, try *paya* soup (goat's trotters).

$$$ Trishna, Sai Baba Marg, next to Commerce House, T022-2261 4991. Good coastal cuisine, seafood, excellent butter garlic crab. Recommended.

$$ Apoorva, near Horniman Circle, Fort, T022-2287 0335. Very good seafood, especially crabs and prawns (downstairs is cheaper).

$$ Britannia, Wakefield House, Sprott Rd, opposite New Custom House, Ballard Estate, T022-22615264. Mon-Sat 1200-1600. Incredible Parsi/Iranian fare with a delicious berry *pullav* made from specially imported Bol berries (cranberries from Iran). Try the *dhansak* and the egg curry. Recommended.

$$ The Excellensea & Bharat Lunch Home, 317 Bharat House, Fort Market, Mint Rd, T022-2261 8991. Excellent seafood and crab as well as *naans* and *rotis*: or try Bombay duck.

$ Lalit, Rustom Sidhwa Rd opposite **Residency Hotel**. Simple but friendly and hygienic pure-veg café, good for South Indian breakfasts, *pav bhaji* in the afternoon, and chai served in dainty china cups. There's a cramped a/c section upstairs.

Around the CST (VT) *p39, map p40*
$$ Badshah Cold Drinks & Snacks, opposite Crawford Market. Famous for its *kulfi* (hand-churned ice cream) and fresh fruit juices (drink without ice), it's a default stop for everyone shopping at Crawford Market. Good and fast *pav-bhaji* (mixed veggies with buttered rolls).

$$ Sadananda, opposite Crawford Market. Excellent south Indian and Gujarati *thalis* and vegetarian food, popular with Indian families.

Marine Drive to Malabar Hill *p41, maps p35 and p40*
$$$ China Garden, Om Chambers, Kemps Corner (at east end of Malabar Hill), T022-3242 3802. Chinese with an Indian hangover. Good food, generous portions, decent alcohol, tables inside and out, no children under 10 allowed inside.

$$$ Gaylord, Vir Nariman Rd, opposite Churchgate. Indian. Good food (huge portions) and service, tables inside and out, barbecue, pleasant, good bar, tempting pastry counter.

$$$ Pearl of the Orient, Ambassador Hotel, T022-2204 1131. This revolving restaurant offers stunning views, especially at night, and very ordinary Chinese food.

$$ Berry's, Vir Nariman Rd, near Churchgate Station, T022-2204 8954. North Indian. Tandoori specialities, good *kulfi*.

$$ Chopsticks, 90A Vir Nariman Rd, Churchgate, T022-2204 9284. Chinese, good, hot and spicy. Offering unusual dishes (*taro* nest, date pancakes, toffee bananas).

$$ Kamling, 82 Vir Nariman Rd, T022-2204 2618. Genuine Cantonese. Simple surroundings, but excellent preparations, try seafood, often busy, even at lunchtime.

$$ Satkar, Indian Express Building, opposite Churchgate station, T022-2204 3259. Indian. Delicious vegetarian, fruit juices and shakes; a/c section more expensive.

$ Purohit's, Vir Nariman Rd, near Churchgate. Indian. Excellent vegetarian *thalis*.

Cafés and snacks

210 Degrees, in Samrat Restaurant complex, Jamshjedji Tata Rd, T022-4213 5407. Superb selection of pure-vegetarian (ie eggless but not vegan) cakes and pastries. Come for afternoon tea as the best stuff is gone by evening.

Tea Centre, 78 Vir Nariman Rd, near Churchgate. Old-fashioned white table cloths and patrons talking in hushed tones make this a throwback to the colonial period, but they do have dozens of light and refreshing tea options, along with a menu of heavy Indian food. Good value and a/c.

Central Mumbai *p43, map p40*

$$$ Goa Portuguesa, THK Rd, Mahim (8 km north of Mumbai Central towards the airport). Authentic dishes, taverna-style with guitarist, try *sungto* (prawn) served between *papads*, *kalwa* (oyster), lobsters cooked with tomatoes, onions and spices and *bebinca* to end the meal.

$$ Swati Snacks, Tardeo Rd, opposite Bhatia Hospital, T022-2352 6411. Gujarati and Parsi snacks along with street foods made in a hygienic fashion: try *khichdi, sev puri, pav bhaji, dahi puri* here. Be prepared for a 20- to 40-min wait, but it's worth it.

$$ Viva Paschim, City View, Dr AB Rd, Worli, T022-2498 3636. Quality coastal Maharashtrian. Sunday lunch buffet great value (Rs 225), folk dances at dinner often.

Bandra, Juhu Beach and Andheri *p44*

$$$ Olive, Union Park, Pali Hill, Bandra, T022-2605 8228. The original **Olive** features wicker furniture in an upscale environment, catering to a cast of characters from Bollywood. Free entry, great pizza and a chic clientele.

$$$ Pali Village Cafe, Ambedkar Rd, Bandra (W), T022-2605 0401. Super-trendy new restaurant done out in shabby-chic industrial style, cascading across different rooms and levels. Good desserts and tapas-style starters, though the wine list and general vibe outweigh the quality of food and service.

$$ Da Vinci, 8 Fatima Villa, 29th Rd, Pali Naka Lane, Bandra West, T022-3248 6033. Italian, one of few sit-down places in Bandra that also serves alcohol. Try the pasta arabiatta and their version of jalapeno peppers. Leave room for dessert.

$$ Gajalee, Kadambari Complex, Hanuman Rd, Vile Parle (E), T022-6692 9592, www.gajalee.com; also in Phoenix Mills. Fine coastal cuisine, try fish tikka, stuffed bombay duck and shellfish with the traditional breads *ghawne* and *amboli*.

$$ Just Around the Corner, 24th-30th road junction, TPS III, Bandra (W). Bright casual American-style diner with all-day salad bar, extensive breakfast menu (0800-1100), and thin crust pizza. Good soup, salad and sandwich combinations.

$$ Out of the Blue, at Union Park, Pali Hill. Steak and fondue, great sizzlers, unusual combinations, flavoured ice teas, flambéed desserts, UV lit inside or outside smoke-free.

$$ Zenzi, Waterfield Rd, Bandra (W). Pan-Asian fusion food, small servings but tasty pork and vegetables. Always packed with a hip media crowd for after-work drinks.

🎵 Bars and clubs

All major hotels and restaurants have bars, others may only serve beer. Most clubs expect couples Fri-Sun, and lone males ('stags' in local parlance) may find it hard to get in. Most pubs charge Rs 350-400 for a 3-litre 'pitcher'; cocktails Rs 400-700. Ask for domestic liquor if you're having vodka or rum cocktails, both Smirnoff and Bacardi are made locally and are half the price. Pick up *Time Out Mumbai*, published every fortnight, for listings and the latest openings, or check http://mumbai.burrp.com.

Bright lights of Bollywood

Mumbai produces around 860 films a year, making Bollywood the world's second largest film-maker after Hong Kong. The stars live in sumptuous dwellings, many of which are on Malabar Hill, Mumbai's Beverley Hills, and despite the spread of foreign videos, their popularity seems to be undiminished.

It is difficult to get permission to visit a studio during filming but you might try **Film City**, Goregaon East, T022-2840 1533 or **Mehboob Studios**, Hill Road, Bandra West, T022-2642 8045. Alternatively, the staff at the Salvation Army Hostel (see Sleeping) may be able to help foreigners get on as 'extras'; Rs 500 per day.

Gateway of India and Colaba *p36, map p37*

Privé, 41/44 Minoo Desai Marg, Colaba, T022-2202 8700. 2130-0130 (weekends until 0230). Rs1000 per couple (Rs 500 for ladies). Slick lounge with hard party music. Serious party-goers with a serious see-and-be-seen scene.
Polly Esther, Gordon House Hotel. A reggae, pop, rock disco, retro-themed club, where anything goes. Open late, most people come here after they finish partying elsewhere.
Woodside Inn, opposite **Regal Cinema** Colaba. Cramped pub carved out of stone Gothic building, with decent retro music, good dining upstairs (pizzas and sandwiches are surprisingly decent) and good selection of whiskies. Free Wi-Fi, too.

Fort *p36, map p37*

Red Light, above **Khyber** (see Eating). Popular with a slightly younger party set, slightly sleazy, always a crowd to get in, 'stags' will find it hard to get in after 2300. Couple entry Rs 1500. DJs rotate, spinning *bhangra*, Top 40, hip hop and Hindi.

Marine Drive to Malabar Hill *p41, map p40*

Dome, Intercontinental Hotel, Marine Dr, T022-6639 9999. Rooftop restaurant and lounge bar with a stunning view of the Queen's Necklace. Try the grilled prawns with your cocktails.

Pizza by the Bay, 143 Marine Dr, T022-2285 1876. Fun place near Churchgate, with live music, karaoke, good food menu (great starters and desserts), generous portions, wide selection of drinks. Loud and lively.

Bandra, Juhu Beach and Andheri *p44*

Aurus, Juhu Tara Rd, Juhu. Trendy seaside patio bar where Bollywood stars rub shoulders with the glitterati. No dance floor, but avant-garde DJs, some international, spin inside. Expensive appetizers, good signature drinks and ocean views. Free entry, easier for couples.
Bling, Leela Hotel (see Sleeping). Club that lives up to its name, stays open late so attracts the spillover from the other clubs. Entry Rs 700-2500 depending on the time, the night, and the bouncers.
China House, Grand Hyatt Hotel, Santa Cruz (E), near domestic airport, T022-6676 1086. High-end Chinese restaurant turns into a happening party after other clubs close around 0130. DJs and music vary. Excellent martinis. Entry Rs 1500 a couple on Fri-Sat.
Hawaiian Shack, 16th Rd, Bandra (W). 1980s bar downstairs, hip hop and dance floor upstairs. Ladies get in free, always crowded.
Toto's, 30th Rd, off Pali Naka, Bandra (W). Retro music, regular clients, and no attitude amid funky automotive decor.
Vie Lounge, Juhu Tara Rd, Juhu. Slightly less attitude than **Aurus** makes this sea-view lounge bar an attractive, but just as pricey, hotspot. Attracts a marginally older crowd.

Mumbai *p33, maps p35, p37 and p40*
Check *TimeOut Mumbai* for upcoming events.

Cinema
Bollywood and international films are screened in dozens of cinemas, most of which are in multiplexes and malls; timings are listed in local news-papers. Multiplexes in South Mumbai include **INOX**, Nariman Point, **Big Cinemas Metro**, southwest corner of Azad Maidan Few independent theatres remain: Try **Eros** opposite Churchgate station, **Regal**, Colaba, or **Sterling**, near CST.

Theatre and classical music
Multilingual Mumbai puts on plays in English, Hindi, Marathi and Gujarati, usually beginning at 1815-1900.
National Centre for Performing Arts, next to Hilton Towers, Nariman Point, T022-6622 3737, www.ncpamumbai.com. Has regular classical music concerts and an Experimental Theatre, which is predictably hit-and-miss.

❂ Festivals and events

Mumbai *p33, maps p35, p37 and p40*
In addition to the national Hindu and Muslim festivals there are the following:
Feb Elephanta Cultural Festival at the caves. Great ambience. Contact MTDC, T022-2202 6713, for tickets Rs 150-200 including launch at 1800. **Kala Ghoda Arts Festival.** Showcase of all forms of fine arts held in various locations around Colaba and Fort. T022-2284 2520.
Mar Jamshed Navroz. This is New Year's Day for the Parsi followers of the Fasli calendar. The celebrations which include offering prayers at temples, exchanging greetings, alms-giving and feasting at home, date back to Jamshed, the legendary King of Persia.
Jul-Aug Janmashtami celebrates the birth of Lord Krishna. Boys and young men form human pyramids and break pots of curd hung up high between buildings.
Aug Coconut Day. The angry monsoon seas are propitiated by devotees throwing coconuts into the ocean.
Aug-Sep Ganesh Chaturthi. Massive figures of Ganesh are towed through the streets to loud techno and storms of coloured powder, before a final *puja* at Chowpatty Beach where they're finally dragged out into the sea. The crowds making their way on foot to the beach cause immense traffic pileups, and the scene at Chowpatty is chaotic, with priests giving *puja* to Ganesh and roaring crowds of men psyching themselves up for the final push into the ocean. A similar celebration happens shortly after at **Durga Pooja** time, when the goddess Durga is worshipped and immersed.
Sep-Oct Dussehra. Group dances by Gujarati women in all the auditoria and residents have their own *garba* and *dandiya* dance nights in the courtyards of their apartment buildings. There are also **Ram leela** celebrations at Chowpatty Beach, where the story of the *Ramayana* is enacted in a dance drama.
Diwali (The Festival of Lights) is particularly popular in mercantile Mumbai when the business community celebrate their New Year and open new account books. **Eid ul-Fitr**, the celebration when Ramzan with its 40 days of fasting is also observed. Since both the Hindu and Islamic calendar are lunar, there is often overlap between the holidays.
25 Dec Christmas. Christians across Mumbai celebrate the birth of Christ. A pontifical High Mass is held at midnight in the open air at the Cooperage Grounds, Colaba.

❂ Shopping

Mumbai *p33, maps p35, p37 and p40*
Most shops are open Mon-Sat 1000-1900, the bazars sometimes staying open as late as 2100. Mumbai prices are often higher than in other Indian cities, and hotel arcades tend to be very pricey but carry good-quality select items. Best buys are textiles, particularly

tie-dye from Gujarat, hand-block printed cottons, Aurangabad and 'Patola' silks, gold-bordered saris from Surat and Khambat, handicrafts, jewellery and leather goods.

It is illegal to take anything over 100 years old out of the country. CDs of contemporary Indian music in various genres make good souvenirs as well as gifts.

Bazars

Crawford Market, Ambedkar Rd (fun for bargain hunting) and **Mangaldas Market**. Other shopping streets are South Bhagat Singh Marg, M Karve Rd and Linking Rd, Bandra. For a different experience try **Chor (Thieves') Bazar**, on Maulana Shaukat Ali Rd in central Mumbai, full of finds from raj leftovers to precious jewellery. Make time to stop at the **Mini Market**, 33-31 Mutton St, T022-2347 2425, minimarket@rediffmail.com (closed Fri), nose through the Bollywood posters, lobby cards, and photo-stills. On Fri, 'junk' carts sell less expensive 'antiques' and fakes.

Books

There are lines of second-hand stalls along Churchgate St and near the University. An annual book fair takes place at the Cross Maidan near Churchgate each Dec. **Crossword**, under the flyover at Kemps Corner bridge (east of Malabar Hill). Smart, spacious, good selection. **Nalanda**, Taj Mahal Hotel. Excellent art books, Western newspapers/magazines. **Strand Books**, off Sir PM Rd near HMV, T022-2206 1994. Excellent selection, best deals, reliable shipping.

Clothes

Benzer, B Desai Rd, Breach Candy. Open daily. Good saris and Indian garments. **The Courtyard**, 41/44 Minoo Desai Marg, Colaba. Very elite and fashionable mini-mall includes boutiques full of stunning heavy deluxe designs (Swarovski crystal-studded saris, anyone?) by Rohit Bal. Rabani & Rakha

(Rs 17,000 for a sari) but probably most suitable to the Western eye is textile designer Neeru Kumar's **Tulsi** label, a cotton textiles designer from Delhi. Beautiful linen/silk stoles and fine *kantha* thread work. There's also a store from top menswear designer Rajesh Pratap Singh. **Ensemble**, 130-132 South Bhagat Singh Marg, T022-2287 2882. Superb craftsmanship and service for women's clothes – Indian and 'East meets West'.

Fabindia, Jeroo Building, 137 M G Rd, Kala Ghoda, and 66 Pali Hill, Bandra, www.fab india.com. Fair-trade handloom Western and Indian wear including *kurtas*, pants, etc, for men, women, children, bamboo, earthenware and jute home furnishings, *khadi* and *mulmul* cloth.

Melange, 33 Altamount Rd, Kemps Corner, T022-2385 4492. Western-tailored, Indian embroidery clothes. Stocks designs from great labels.

Crafts and textiles

Government emporia from many states sell good handicrafts and textiles; several at **World Trade Centre**, Cuffe Parade. In Colaba, a street **Craft Market** is held on Sun (Nov-Jan) in K Dubash Marg.

Anokhi, 4B August Kranti Marg, opposite Kumbala Hill Hospital. Gifts and handicrafts. **Bombay Electric**, 1 Reay House, BEST Marg, Colaba, T022-2287 6276, www.bombayelectric.in. Pricey, chic, trendsetter art and couture.

Bombay Store, Western India House, 1st floor, PM Rd, Fort, www.bombaystore.com. Open daily. Ethnic lifestyle supplies, from home decor and fancy paper to clothing, gifts, best one-stop shop, value for money. **Cottage Industries Emporium**, Apollo Bunder, Colaba. A nationwide selection, especially Kashmiri embroidery, South Indian handicrafts and Rajasthani textiles. Colaba Causeway, next to **BEST**, for ethnic ware, handicrafts and fabrics.

Curio Cottage, 19 Mahakavi Bhushan Rd, near the Regal Cinema, Colaba, T022-2202 2607. Silver jewellery and antiques.
Good Earth, 104 Kemp's Corner and Raghuvanshi Mills, Lower Parel. Smart, trendy, pottery, glass homewares.
Natesan in Jehangir Gallery basement; also in **Taj Hotel**. For fine antiques and copies.
Phillips, Madame Cama Rd, Colaba. An Aladdin's cave of bric-a-brac and curios. Pricey.
Sadak Ali, behind **Taj Hotel**, Colaba. Good range of carpets, but bargain hard.
Yamini, President House, Wodehouse Rd, Colaba, especially for vibrant textiles.

Electronics
DN Rd between Flora Fountain and CST has mobile and camera shops every few steps, but prices for genuine goods are not particularly low. There are a few second-hand camera shops towards CST. If buying new equipment, ask for a bill and international warranty.
Croma, Horniman Circle; also at Phoenix Mills, Lower Parel. Electronics store for cameras, phones and USB drives.
Heera Panna Shopping Arcade, Haji Ali. Formerly the grey-market for smuggled electrical goods, now mostly above board.

Jewellery
In Bandra, Turner Rd has about 10 jewellery stores in a row to cater to every price range and taste – from traditional Indian styles to contemporary updates in gold, diamonds, and other precious and semi-precious stones. The **Cottage Industries Emporium**, near Radio Club, Colaba Causeway, has excellent silver and antique jewellery from across India.
Popli Suleman Chambers, Battery St, Apollo Bunder, Colaba, T022-2285 4757. Semi-precious stones, gems, garnets and pearls.

Music
Musical instruments on VB Patel Rd, **RS Mayeka** at No 386, **Haribhai Vishwanath** at No 419 and Ram Singh at Bharati Sadan.

Hiro, Hill Rd, Bandra. Good Indian classical CDs.
Planet M, opposite CST station; smaller branches in most malls. Also has book/poetry readings, gigs.
Rhythm House, next to Jehangir Gallery. Excellent selection of jazz and classical CDs. Also sells tickets for classical concerts.

Silks and saris
Many places including **Kala Niketan**, MG Rd and **Juhu Reclamation**.
Biba, next to Crossword, Kemp's Corner, Phoenix Mills, Lower Parel, Bandra (W). Affordable designer wear for ladies, alterations possible.
Nalli, Shop No 7, Thirupathi Apartments, Bhulabhai Desai Rd, T022-23535577. Something for every budget.
Ritu Kumar, Turner Rd, Bandra (W), Phoenix Mills, Lower Parel, Bandra (W), Ethnic and Western designer wear for ladies, including very contemporary silk T-shirts.
Sheetal, Tirupati Apartments, B Desai Rd. Saris from all over India; fair prices.

▲▲ Activities and tours

Mumbai *p33, maps p35, p37 and p40*
Adventure tourism
Maharashtra Tourism, www.maharashtra tourism.gov.in. Actively encourages adventure tourism (including jungle safaris and water sports) by introducing 'rent-a-tent' and hiring out trekking gear, and organizing overnight trips; some accommodation comes with. Prices range from US$35-150 per day/weekend depending on season and activity. It has also set up 27 holiday resorts around the state providing cheap accommodation at hill stations, beaches, archaeological sites and scenic spots. Details from tourist offices.
Odati Adventures, T(0)9820-079802, www.odati.com. Camping, weekend hiking, bike rides, rock climbing and waterfall rappelling around the Mumbai area. If you go rappelling in Maljesh Ghat during the

monsoon, you'll glimpse thousands of flamingos. Bikes can be hired. Call or book online. Weekend cycle tours are Rs 2000-3000.

Body and soul

Iyengar Yogashraya, Emac House, 126 Senapati Bapat Marg (off Tulsi Pipe road opposite Kamla Mills), Lower Parel, T022-2494 8416, www.bksiyengar.com. Iyengar drop-in centre. Call before dropping in.
Kaivalyadahama, next to Taraporewala Aquarium, Marine Dr.
Kerala Ayurvedic Health Spa, Prabhadevi, next to Subway and Birdy's, T022-6520 7445. Very reasonable rates for massage, Rs 900 for 45 mins. Call for an appointment.
Yoga Institute, Praghat Colony, Santa Cruz (E). T022-2611 0506.
Yoga Training Centre, 51 Jai Hind Club, Juhu Scheme, T022-2649 9020.
Yoga Vidhya Niketan, Sane Guruji Marg, Dadar, T022-2430 6258.

Horse racing

Mahalaxmi Race Course, opposite Haji Ali. Season Nov-Mar, Sun and holidays, 1400-1700. Many of India's top races are held at the delightful course (1878), including the Derby in Feb/Mar. Check newspapers for listings.

Tour operators

If you wish to sightsee independently with a guide, ask at the tourist office. See page 33.
Be the Local, T(0)9930-027370, www.bethe localtoursandtravels.com. Fascinating walking tours of Dharavi, which take you through some of the cottage industries – from traditional Gujarati pottery to plastic – which sustain Mumbai from within Asia's largest slum. Owned and run by local students, the tours are neither voyeuristic nor intrusive, and photography is prohibited. Rs 400 per person includes transport from Colaba; private tours Rs 3500 for up to 5 people.
Bombay Heritage Walks, T022-2369 0992, www.bombayheritagewalks.com. Informative

walking tours specializing in Mumbai's built history, founded by a pair of local architects.
City sightseeing Approved guides from the India tourist office, T022-2203 6854. City tour usually includes visits to The Gateway of India, the Chhatrapati Shivaji (Prince of Wales) Museum, Jain temple, Hanging Gardens, Kamla Nehru Park and Mani Bhavan (Gandhi Museum). Suburban tour includes Juhu Beach, Kanheri Caves and Lion Safari Park.
MTDC, Madam Cama Rd, opposite LIC Building, T022-2202 6713. City tour Tue-Sun 0900-1300 and 1400-1800, Rs 100. Suburban tour 0915 (from Dadar 1015-1815. Fort walk is a heritage walk around CST and Fort area with the Kala Ghoda Association, Army & Navy Building, T022-2285 2520, www.artindia.co.in. Elephanta tours from Gateway of India. Boat, 0900-1415, Rs 70 return; reserve at Apollo Bunder, T022-2202 6364.
Mumbai Magic, T(0)98677-07414, www.mumbaimagic.com. Deepa Krishnan and her army of erudite guides offer a vast range of tours covering every inch of the city from Colaba to Bandra and beyond. Highlights include South Indian cuisine tours of Matunga, a walk through the Chor Bazaar, and the Mumbai Local tour which hops you around the city by taxi, local train and bus. Personalised itineraries available. Professional and highly recommended.

Travel agents **Cox and Kings**, 16 Bank St, Fort, T022-2270 9100; **Everett**, 1 Regent Chambers, Nariman Pt, T022-2204 8141; **Mercury**, 70VB Gandhi Rd, T022-6615 3477; **Space Travels**, 4th floor, Sir PM Rd, T022-2266 2481, for discounted flights and special student offers, Mon-Fri 1000-1700, Sat 1030-1500; **TCI**, 324 Dr DN Rd, Fort, T022-6160 3333; **Thomas Cook**, Cooks Building, Dr DN Rd, T1800-209 9100; **Venture**, ground floor, Abubakar Mansion, Shahid Bhagat Singh Marg, T022-2287 6666, efficient, helpful.

Mumbai *p33, maps p35, p37 and p40*
Mumbai is one of the 2 main entry points to India, with daily international flights from Europe, North America, the Middle East, Asia, Australia and Africa, and frequent domestic connections with every major city in India, and most minor ones. All touch down at **Chhatrapati Shivaji International Airport**, enquiries T022-6685 0222, www.csia.in. The recently smartened-up international terminal is 30 km north of the city. There are exchange counters, ATMs, tourist offices, domestic airline and railway reservation counters, and a cloakroom for left luggage.

Domestic, recently renovated with 2 separate terminals – 1A for **Air India** and **Kingfisher** (enquiries T022-6685 1351), 1B for **Jet Airways** and all budget airlines (enquiries T022-2626 1149), is 4 km closer to the city in Santa Cruz and has most of the same facilities. Free shuttle buses link the domestic and international terminals every few mins.

Transport to and from the airport
Pre-paid taxis, from counters at the exits, are the simplest way of getting downtown. Give the exact area or hotel and the number of pieces of luggage, and pay at the booth. On the receipt will be scribbled the number of your taxi: ask the drivers outside to help you find it, and hand the receipt to the driver at the end of the journey. There is no need to tip, though drivers will certainly drop heavy hints. To **Nariman Point** or **Gateway of India**, about Rs 430, 1-2 hrs depending on traffic. To **Juhu Beach** Rs 290. Metered taxis picked up outside the terminal should be marginally cheaper than a pre-paid, but make sure the driver starts the meter when you get in. The cheaper alternatives – crowded and slow **BEST** buses that connect both terminals with the city, and even more crowded local **trains** – have only economy in their favour. The closest railway stations are **Vile Parle**

(for International) and **Santa Cruz** (Domestic), both on the Western line to Mumbai Central and Churchgate.

Airline offices
Domestic The easiest way to comparison shop for domestic fares is online, though not all sites accept international credit cards. One that does is www.cleartrip.com.

Air India (Indian Airlines), Jet Airways and **Kingfisher** are full-service airlines and have the most comprehensive networks; budget carriers such as **Go Air**, **Indigo** and **Spicejet** serve major routes and charge for extras. During the winter, prepare for a 'congestion charge' on certain domestic routes, including Mumbai–Delhi.

Air India, Nariman Pt, T022-2202 3031, www.airindia.com, to all major cities. **Go Air**, T(0)9223-222111, T1800-222 111, www.go air.in. **Indigo**, T(0)9910-383838, T1800-180 3838, www.goindigo.in. **Jet Airways**, T022-3989 3333, www.jetairways.com. **Kingfisher**, T(0)9910-383838, www.fly kingfisher.com. **Spicejet**, T1800-180 3333, T(0)9871-803333, www.spicejet.com.

International Air India, 1st floor, Nariman Pt (counters also at Taj Mahal Hotel and airports), T022-2758 0777, airport T022-2615 6633. **Air Canada**, Amarchand Mansions, Madam Cama Rd, T022-2202 0597. **Air France**, Sarjan Plaza, 100 Annie Besant Rd, Worli, T022-2202 4818, airport T022-2682 8072. **British Airways**, 202-B Vulcan Ins Building, Vir Nariman Rd, T1800-1023 5922, Mon-Fri 0800-1300, 1345-1800. Sat 0900-1300. **Emirates**, Mittal Chamber, Nariman Pt, T022-4097 4097. **Gulf Air**, Maker Chambers, 5 Nariman Pt, T022-2202 1626. **Interglobe**, ground floor, Podar House, Sitaram D Marg, Marine Dr, T022 6137 0808, handles enquiries for China Eastern, Delta, SAS, South African, and United. **Japan**, Raheja Centre, Nariman Pt, T022-2283 3215. **KLM**, Sarjan Plaza, 100 Annie Besant Rd, Worli, T022-6685 9174. **Kuwait**, 9th floor, Nariman

Bhavan, Nariman Point, T022-6655 5655.
Lufthansa, Express Towers, Nariman Pt, T022-2682 9898. **PIA**, Mittal Towers, Nariman Pt, T022-2202 1598. **Qantas**, 4th floor, Sunteck Centre, 37-40 Subhash Rd, Vile Parle (East), T022-6111 1818. **Royal Jordanian**, Dalamal Tower, Nariman Point, T022-2202 2779. **Singapore Airlines**, Taj Intercontinental, T022-2202 2747. **Sri Lankan**, Raheja Centre, Nariman Pt, T022-2284 4148, airport T022-2832 7050. **Thai Airways**, 15 World Trade Centre, Cuffe Parade, T022-6637 3737.

Bus
Local Red **BEST** (Brihanmumbai Electrical Supply Co) buses are available in most parts of Greater Mumbai. There's a handy route finder at http://bestundertaking.com/transport/index.htm. Fares are cheap, but finding the correct bus is tricky as the numbers and destinations on the front are only in Marathi. English signs are displayed beside the back doors. Ask locals to help point out a bus going your way.

Long distance Maharashtra SRTC operates from the Mumbai Central Bus Stand, T022-2307 4272, http://msrtconline.in/timetable.aspx, to most major centres in the state as well as interstate destinations including **Ahmedabad**, **Bengaluru** (**Bangalore**), **Goa**, **Mangalore**, **Indore**, **Vadodara** and **Hyderabad**. Buses to **Nashik** and **Pune** leave from the more inconvenient stand on Senapati Bapat Marg, north of the centre in Dadar, T022-2430 2667.

Private buses also serve long-distance destinations: most leave from the streets surrounding Mumbai Central, where there are ticket agents, while others leave from Dadar; information and tickets from **Dadar Tourist Centre**, outside Dadar station, T022-2411 3398. The most popular company is **Neeta Volvo**, T022-2411 6114. Some private buses can be booked in advance on www.redbus.in.

Car
Costs for hiring a car are (for 8 hrs or 80 km): luxury a/c cars Rs 1500; Maruti/Ambassador, a/c Rs 1000, non-a/c Rs 800. Companies include: **Auto Hirers**, 7 Commerce Centre, Tardeo, T022-2494 2006. **Blaze**, Colaba, T022-2202 0073. **Budget**, T022-2494 2644, and **Sai**, Phoenix Mill Compound, Senapati Bapat Marg, Lower Parel, T022-2494 2644. Recommended. **NRI Services**, Chowpatty, T(0)9821-252287, www.nriservicesindia.com. **Wheels**, T022-2282 2874.

Auto-rickshaw
Not available in central Mumbai (south of Mahim). Metered; about Rs 9 per km, revised tariff card held by the driver, 25% extra at night (2400-0500). Some rickshaw drivers show the revised tariff card for taxis!

Taxi
Metered yellow-top cabs and more expensive a/c Cool Cabs are easily available. Meter rates are Rs 16 for the 1st kilometre and Rs 10 for each extra kilometre. Drivers should carry tariff cards that convert the meter fee into current prices; a new fleet of yellow-top Indica cars have digital meters that show the correct price. Always get a pre-paid taxi at the airport.

A/c radio taxis can be pre-booked. They charge Rs 15 per km and provide metered receipts at the end of your journey. Tip the driver about 10 percent if you feel they had to do a lot of waiting. **Megacab**, T022-4242 4242. **Meru Cab**, T022-4422 4422.

Train
Local Suburban electric trains are economical. They start from Churchgate for the western suburbs and CST (**VT**) for the east but are often desperately crowded; stay near the door or you may miss your stop. There are 'ladies' cars' in the middle and ends. Avoid peak hours (south-bound 0700-1100, northbound 1700-2000), and keep a tight hold on valuables. The difference between

1st and 2nd class is not always obvious although 1st class is 10 times as expensive. Inspectors fine people for travelling in the wrong class or without a ticket. If you're travelling frequently, invest in a smart card that lets you avoid queues at the ticket counter by printing tickets from a machine.

Long distance Times for trains are published each Sat in the *Indian Express* paper. Mumbai is the HQ of the **Central and Western Railways**, CST, enquiries, T134/135; reservations, T022-2265 9512, 0800-1230, 1300-1630 (Foreigners' Counter opens 0900; best time to go). **Western Railway**, at Churchgate and Mumbai Central, 0800-1345, 1445-2000. All stations have a Foreign Tourist counter for Indrail Passes and Foreign Tourist Quota bookings; bring your passport and an ATM receipt or encashment certificate.

The following depart from **CST** unless specified by these abbreviations: **Bandra (B)**, **Central (C)**, **Dadar (D)**, **Lokmanya Tilak (LT)**: **Ahmedabad** (all from Mumbai Central): *Shatabdi Exp 12009*, 0625, except Fri, 7 hrs; *Karnavati Exp 12933*, 1340, except Wed, 7¾ hrs; *Saurashtra Mail 19005*, 2025, 9 hrs; *Gujarat Mail 12901*, 2150, 9 hrs. **Allahabad**: *Kolkata Mail 12322*, 2125, 23½ hrs; *Mahanagari Exp 11093*, 2355, 24¼ hrs. **Agra Cantonment**: *Punjab Mail 12137*, 1910, 21½ hrs. **Aurangabad** (for **Ajanta** and **Ellora**): *Tapovan Exp 17617*, 0610, 7½ hrs; *Devgiri Exp 17057*, 1205, 7½ hrs. **Bengaluru (Bangalore)**: *Udyan Exp 16529*, 0755, 24¾ hrs; *Coimbatore Exp 11013*, 2220 (**LT**), 23¾ hrs. **Bhopal**: *Pushpak Exp 12133*, 0810, 14 hrs; *Punjab Mail 12137*, 1910, 14 hrs. **Chennai**: *Dadar Chennai Exp 11063*, 2020 (**D**), 23¾ hrs; *Chennai Exp 11041*, 1400, 26¾ hrs. **Ernakulam (Kochi)**: *Netravati Exp 16345*, 2300 (**LT**), 29½ hrs. **Guntakal** (for **Hospet/Hampi**): *Dadar Chennai Exp 11063*, 2020 (**D**), 15 hrs; *Udyan Exp 16529*, 0755, 16¾ hrs; *Coimbatore Exp 11013*, 2220 (**LT**), 16¼ hrs; *Kanniyakumari Exp 11081*, 1535,

17¾ hrs. **Gwalior**: *Punjab Mail 12137*, 1910, 19¾ hrs. **Hyderabad**: *Hussainsagar Exp 17001*, 2155, 15¼ hrs; *Hyderabad Exp 17031*, 1235, 17½ hrs. **Kolkata (Howrah)**: *Gitanjali Exp 12859*, 0600, 33 hrs; *Howrah Mail 18001*, 2015, 35½ hrs. **Lucknow**: *Pushpak Exp 12133*, 0810, 25½ hrs.

Madgaon (for **Goa**): The day train is a good option, the night service is heavily booked. Special trains during the winter high season. *Mandavi Exp 10103*, 0515, 11 hrs; *Konkan Kanya Exp 10111*, 2240, 12 hrs; *Netravati Exp 16345*, 1140, 13½ hrs (**LT**). **New Delhi**: *Rajdhani Exp 12951*, 1655 (**C**), 17 hrs; *Golden Temple Mail 12903*, 2130 (**C**), 21½ hrs; *August Kranti Rajdhani Exp 12953*, 1740 (**C**), 17¼ hrs (to Hazrat Nizamuddin). **Pune**: deluxe trains *Shatabdi Exp 12027*, 0640, 3½ hrs; *Deccan Queen Exp 12123*, 1710, 3½ hrs, among many. **Thiruvananthapuram**: *Netravati Exp 16345*, 1140 (**LT**), 35 hrs. **Ujjain**: *Avantika Exp 12961*, 1925 (**C**), 12½ hrs. **Varanasi**: *Lokmanya Tilak Varanasi Exp 12165*, 0520 (**LT**), Mon, Thu, Sat, 26 hrs; *Muzaffarpur/Darbanga Exp 11061*, 1215 (**LT**), 27¼ hrs.

❶ Directory

Mumbai *p33, maps p35, p37 and p40*
Banks ATMS are now ubiquitous in all parts of the city, including at the airports and stations, and most take foreign cards. For other services, branches open Mon-Fri 1000-1400, Sat 1000-1200. It's more efficient to change money at the airport, or at specialist agents, eg **Bureau de Change**, upstairs in Air India Building, Nariman Pt; **Thomas Cook**, 324 Dr DN Rd, T022-2204 8556; also at 102B Maker Tower, 10th floor, F Block, Cuffe Pde, Colaba. **Credit cards American Express**, Oriental Bldg, 364 Dr DN Rd; **Diners Club**, Raheja Chambers, 213 Nariman Pt; **MasterCard**, C Wing, Mittal Tower, Nariman Pt; **Visa**, Standard Chartered Grindlays Bank, 90 MG Rd, Fort. **Embassies and consulates** Australia, 36 Maker

Chambers VI, Nariman Point, T022-6116 7100. **Austria**, Maker Chambers VI, Nariman Pt, T022-2285 1066. **France**, Datta Prasad, NG Cross Rd, T022-2495 0918. **Canada**, 6th floor, 221 Dr DN Rd, T022-6749 4444. **Germany**, 10th floor, Hoechst House, Nariman Pt, T022-2283 2422. **Indonesia**, 19 Altamount Rd, T022-2386 8678. **Israel**, 50 Deshmukh Marg, Kailas, T022-2386 2794. **Italy**, Kanchenjunga, 72G Deshmukh Marg, T022-2380 4071. **Japan**, 1 ML Dahanukar Marg, T022-2493 4310. **Malaysia**, Rahimtoola House, Homji St, T022-2266 0056. **Netherlands**, 1 Marine Lines Cross Rd, Churchgate, T022-2201 6750. **Philippines** , Sekhar Bhavan, Nariman Pt, T022-2281 4103. **Spain**, 6 K Dubash Marg, T022-2287 4797. **Sri Lanka**, 34 Homi Modi St, T022-2204 5861. **Sweden**, 85 Sayani Rd, Prabhadevi, T022-2421 2681. **Thailand**, 43 B Desai Rd, T022-2363 1404. **UK**, Naman Chambers, C/32 G Block, Bandra Kurla Complex, Bandra (E), T022-6650 2222. **USA**, Lincoln House, B Desai Rd, T022-2363 3611 (24 hrs). **Emergencies** Ambulance T102. Fire T101. Police T100. **Internet** Internet cafés are increasingly strict about demanding photo ID. There are several on the back streets of Colaba near Leopold Café: **I-way**, corner of Colaba Causeway and Barrow Rd (near Kamat restaurant), has many terminals and fast access; you must first register as a member but it's well worth it, and there are branches throughout India. **Infotek**, Express Towers, ground floor, Nariman Pt. **British Council**, A Wing, 1st floor, Mittal Tower, Nariman Pt, T022-2282 3560, 1000-1745, Tue-Sat. **Cybercafé**, Waterfield, Bandra, enjoy coffee and cake while you surf, take government-issued ID to access free Wi-Fi; a number of bars and cafés now offer Wi-Fi access free or by pre-paid voucher, including **Woodside Inn**, opposite Regal Cinema, Colaba, and **Banyan Tree Café and Bakery**, opposite Podar Hospital, Worli (north of Haji Ali), T022-6452 7222. **Medical services** The larger hotels usually have a house doctor, the others invariably have a doctor on call. Ask hotel staff for prompt action. The telephone directory lists hospitals and GPs. Admission to private hospitals may not be allowed without a large cash advance (eg Rs 50,000). Insurers' guarantees may not be sufficient. **Prince Aly Khan Hospital**, Nesbit Rd near the harbour, T022-2377 7800/900, Jaslok Hospital on Peddar Rd, T022-6657 3333; Hinduja Hospital T022-2444-0431; Lilavati Hospital in Bandra (W), T022-2642 1111 are recommended. Chemists: several open day/ night especially opposite Bombay Hospital. **Wordell**, Stadium House, Churchgate; **New Royal Chemist**, New Marine Lines.

Post Nagar Chowk, Mon-Sat 0900-2000 (Poste Restante facilities 0900-1800) and Sun 1000-1730; parcels from 1st floor, rear of building, Mon-Sat 1000-1700; cheap 'parcelling' service on pavement outside; Colaba PO, Henry Rd, 2 blocks south of Taj Mahal. Counter at Domestic airport. **Useful contacts** Commissioner's Office, Dr DN Rd, near Phule Market. **Foreigners' Regional Registration Office**, 3rd floor, Special Branch Building, Badruddin Tayabji Lane, Behind St Xaviers College, T022-2262 1169. **Passport office**, T022-2493 1731.

Around Mumbai

The Hindu caves of Elephanta and the Buddhist caves of Kanheri
are within easy reach of the city. You can also cross the bay to
Chaul to the south, or head for the sandy beaches at Kihim. The
old Portuguese fort of Bassein is to the north, while up in the hills
lies the cool, car-free refuge of Matheran.

Elephanta Caves → *For listings, see pages 65-66.*

The heavily forested **Elephanta Island**, barely visible in the haze from Mumbai, rises out of the bay like a giant whale only 10 km away. The setting is symbolically significant; the sea is the ocean of life, a world of change (Samsara) in which is set an island of spiritual and physical refuge. The 'caves', excavated over 1000 years ago in the volcanic lava high up the slope of the hill, saw Hindu craftsmen express their view of spiritual truths in massive carvings of extraordinary grace. Sadly a large proportion have been severely damaged, but enough remains to illustrate something of their skill.

History
The vast majority of India's 1200 **cave sites** were created as temples and monasteries between the third century BC and the 10th century AD. Jain, Buddhist and Hindu caves often stand side by side. The temple cave on Elephanta Island, dedicated to Siva, was probably excavated during the eighth century by the Rashtrakuta Dynasty which ruled the Deccan AD 757-973, though the caves may have had earlier Buddhist origins. An earlier name for the island was Garhapuri ('city of forts') but the Portuguese renamed it after the colossal sculpted elephants when they captured Mumbai from the Sultan of Gujarat in 1535, and stationed a battalion there. They reportedly used the main pillared cave as a shooting gallery causing some of the damage you see. Muslim and British rulers were not blameless either.

Ins and outs
The site is open Tuesday to Sunday, sunrise to sunset; foreigners Rs 250, Indians Rs 10, plus Rs 5 passenger tax. Weekends are very busy. From the landing place, a 300 m unshaded path along the quayside and then about 110 rough steps lead to the caves at a height of 75 m. The walk along the quay can be avoided when the small train functions (Rs 8 return). The climb can be trying for some, especially if it is hot, though *doolies* (chairs carried by porters) are available for Rs 300 return, Rs 200 one-way. At the start of the climb there are stalls selling refreshments, knick-knacks and curios (including models of the Eiffel Tower), but if you're carrying food watch out for aggressive monkeys. **Maharashtra Tourism** normally organizes a festival of classical music and dance on the island in the third week of February. Early morning is the best time for light and also for avoiding large groups with guides which arrive from 1000. The caves tend to be quite dark so carry a powerful torch.

The site

Entrance Originally there were three entrances and 28 pillars at the site. The entrances on the east and west have subsidiary shrines which may have been excavated and used for different ceremonies. The main entrance is now from the north. At dawn, the rising sun casts its rays on the approach to the *garbagriha* (main shrine), housed in a square structure at the west end of the main hall. On your right is a carving of Siva as Nataraj. On the left he appears as Lakulisa in a much damaged carving. Seated on a lotus, the Buddha-like figure is a symbol of the unconscious mind and enlightenment, found also in Orissan temples where Lakulisa played a prominent role in attempting to attract Buddhists back into Hinduism. From the steps at the entrance you can see the *yoni-lingam*, the symbol of the creative power of the deity.

Main Hall The ribbed columns in the main hall, 5-6 m high and in a cruciform layout, are topped by a capital. At the corner of each pillar is a dwarf signifying *gana* (the earth spirit), and sometimes the figure of Ganesh (Ganapati). To the right, the main **Linga Shrine** has four entrances, each corresponding to a cardinal point guarded by a *dvarpala*. The sanctum is bare, drawing attention to the *yonilingam* which the devotee must walk around clockwise.

Wall panels To the north of the main shrine is **Bhairava killing the demon Andhakasura**. This extraordinarily vivid carving shows Siva at his most fearsome, with a necklace of skulls, crushing the power of Andhaka, the Chief of Darkness. It was held that if he was wounded each drop of his blood would create a new demon. So Siva impaled him with his sword and collected his blood with a cup, which he then offered to his wife Shakti. In winter this panel is best seen in the early afternoon.

Opposite, on the south side of the main shrine is the damaged panel of **Kalyan Sundari**, in which Siva stands with Parvati on his right, just before their wedding (normally a Hindu wife stands on her husband's left). She looks down shyly, but her body is drawn to him. Behind Parvati is her father Himalaya and to his left Chandramas, the moon god carrying a gift – *soma*, the food of the gods. On Siva's left is Vishnu and below him Brahma.

At the extreme west end of the temple are **Nataraja** (left) and **Yogisvara Siva** (right). The former shows a beautiful figure of Ganesh above and Parvati on his left. All the other gods watch him. Above his right shoulder is the four-headed God of Creation, Brahma. Below Brahma is the elephant-headed Ganesh.

On the south wall, opposite the entrance are three panels. **Gangadhara** is on the west. The holy River Ganga (Bhagirathi) flowed only in heaven but was brought to earth by her father King Bhagiratha (kneeling at Siva's right foot). Here, Ganga is shown in the centre, flanked by her two tributaries, Yamuna and Saraswati. These three rivers are believed to meet at Allahabad.

To the left of these is the centre piece of the whole temple, the remarkable **Mahesvara**, the Lord of the Universe. Here Siva is five-headed, for the usual triple-headed figure has one face looking into the rock and another on top of his head. Nearly 6 m high, he unites all the functions of creation, preservation and destruction. Some see the head on the left (your right) as representing Vishnu, the Creator, while others suggest that it shows a more feminine aspect of Siva. To his right is Rudra or Bhairava, with snakes in his hair, a skull to represent ageing from which only Siva is free, and he has a look of anger. The central face is Siva as his true self, Siva Swarupa, balancing out creation and destruction. In this mode

India's first railway line

The opening of India's first railway line from Mumbai to Thane in 1853 prepared the route through the Ghats to the Deccan Plateau. Mumbai became the hub of regional and international trade. Victoria Terminus (CST now) was the product of a magnificent era of railway building at the end of the 19th century when the British Raj was striding confidently towards the 20th century.

With the disappearance of the East India Company after the Mutiny, the Government of India took over the responsibility for running the railways. On 16 April 1853 the first train made its run from Mumbai along 32 km of line to Thane. Subsequent advances were rapid but often incredible natural obstacles presented great challenges to the railway builders. The 263-km line to Surat encountered 18 rivers and some of the foundations for the bridges had to be driven 45 m in to the ground to cope with the monsoon floodwaters.

he is passive and serene, radiating peace and wisdom like the Buddha. His right hand is held up in a calming gesture and in his left hand is a lotus bud.

The panel to the left has the **Ardhanarisvara**. This depicts Siva as the embodiment of male and female, representing wholeness and the harmony of opposites. The female half is relaxed and gentle, the mirror in the hand symbolizing the woman reflecting the man. Siva has his 'vehicle', Nandi on the right.

To the east, opposite the *garbha-griha*, was probably the original entrance. On the south is Siva and Parvati **Playing chaupar on Mount Kailash**. Siva is the faceless figure. Parvati has lost and is sulking but her playful husband persuades her to return to the game. They are surrounded by Nandi, Siva's bull, celestial figures and an ascetic with his begging bowl.

On the north is **Ravana Shaking Mount Kailash** on which Siva is seated. Siva is calm and unperturbed by Ravana's show of brute strength and reassures the frightened Parvati. He pins down Ravana with his toe, who fails to move the mountain and begs Siva's forgiveness which is granted.

Chaul, Kihim and Alibag beaches → *For listings, see pages 65-66.*

A group of Moorish and Portuguese forts lie to the south at the mouth of Mumbai harbour. **Chaul** was taken in 1522 by the Portuguese. Similar to Bassein with a very attractive fort, it never equalled it in importance. The Marathas took it in 1739 and in 1818 it passed into British hands. Little remains of the settlement apart from ruined churches and broken walls. If you look across the creek you will see the hilltop Muslim fort of Korlai. The clean beach, safe waters and very pleasant surroundings make **Kihim** very attractive but the summer sun can be murderously hot. The beach is muddy at **Alibag** and it is possible to walk across to the fort at low tide but it is not worth the Rs 100 entrance fee. If you decide to stay, there are a few places on Kihim Beach.

Kanheri Caves → *For listings, see pages 65-66.*

Sanjay Gandhi National Park, north of the city at Goregaon, is worth a visit in itself for its dense deciduous and semi-evergreen forest providing a beautiful habitat for several varieties of deer, antelope, butterflies, birds and the occasional leopard. However, the main reason for visiting is for the **Kanheri Caves** situated in the heart of the park.

Some 42 km north of Mumbai, the caves (also known as Mahakali Caves) are on a low hill midway between Borivli and Thane. The hills used to form the central part of Salsette Island, but the surrounding land has long since been extensively built on. Further up the ravine from the caves there are some fine views across the Bassein Fort and out to sea. Still shaded by trees, the entrance is from the south. There are 109 Buddhist caves, dating from the end of the second to the ninth century AD with flights of steps joining them. The most significant is the **Chaitya Cave** (cave 3) circa sixth century. The last Hinayana chaitya hall to be excavated is entered through a forecourt and veranda. The pillared entrance has well carved illustrations of the donors, and the cave itself comprises a 28 m x 13 m colonnaded hall of 34 pillars. At one end these encircle the 5-m-high *dagoba*. Some of the pillars have carvings of elephants and trees. Fifty metres up the ravine is **Darbar of the Maharajah Cave** (Cave 10). This was a *dharamshala* (resthouse) and has two stone benches running down the sides and some cells leading off the left and back walls. Above Cave 10 is **Cave 35** which was a *vihara* (monastery), which has reliefs of a Buddha seated on a lotus and of a disciple spreading his cloak for him to walk on. All the caves have an elaborate drainage and water storage system, fresh rainwater being led into underground storage tanks.

Above the cave complex is **Ashok Van**, a sacred grove of ancient trees, streams and springs. From there, a three-hour trek leads to 'View Point', the highest in Mumbai. There are breathtaking views. Photography is prohibited from the radar station on top of the hill; there are excellent opportunities just below it.

The park is also home to hyena and panther, though rarely seen, while three lakes have ducks, herons and crocodiles. Nature trails lead from Film City (reached by bus from Goregaon station). A lion safari leaves from **Hotel Sanjay** near Borivli station.

North Konkan → *For listings, see pages 65-66.*

The undulating lowland of the North Konkan coast forms a narrow strip between the Arabian Sea and the often daunting west facing slopes of the Ghats. There are occasional good beaches, scattered mangrove swamps, and rice growing valleys, interspersed with poor laterite covered hills. The beaches to the north, a two-hour journey away, make them a popular getaway from Mumbai, although foreign tourists are virtually unheard of. The beaches can't compare to those of Goa or Kerala and litter and other debris is all too evident.

Bassein (Vasai)

Bassein, at the mouth of the Ulhas River on the mainland, is 60 km north of central Mumbai. Due to silting, the fort on the Bassein Creek is now some distance from the sea. The structure is in ruins, but it is well worth walking round the sea face. Originally built by Bahadur Shah, Sultan of Gujarat, it was one of a chain of forts against the Portuguese. However, the chain was breached, and the Portuguese remodelled the city along their own lines, renaming it **Vasai**. From 1534 to 1739 it became so prosperous as a centre of shipbuilding and the export of Bassein stone that it was called the Court of the North. As a walled city it contained a cathedral, five convents, 13 churches and the splendid houses and palaces of the aristocracy, or Hidalgos, who with members of the religious orders, alone were allowed to live within the walls. The Marathas took Vasai in February 1739 after a long and desperate siege. Almost the whole Portuguese garrison, 800 strong, was killed in the battle; the Marathas are thought to have lost 5000 men. In 1780 the British evicted the Marathas, only to return it to them three years later under the Treaty of Salbai.

Approached from the north, the fort in the town contains the ruins of St Joseph's Cathedral (1536), St Anthony's, the Jesuit church and the convents, all belonging to Franciscans, Dominicans, Jesuits or Augustinians. **Nalasopara**, 10 km northwest, is the ancient Konkan capital where Buddhist relics have been found.

The Ghats → *For listings, see pages 65-66.*

The Ghats represent an historic divide between the outward looking coastal lowlands with the trading centre of Mumbai at their hub, and the much drier interior, a battle ground of successive Indian dynasties. Today the hilltops are littered with fortified sites, while hill stations offer weekend breaks to Mumbai's elite. The routes through the Western Ghats from Mumbai climb to nearly 1600 m through the forested slopes, particularly beautiful before the end of the rains in September when wild flowers are everywhere, and rivers and waterfalls are full. Road travel is often disrupted in the rains, but the railways through the Ghats are spectacular. On the Nashik route alone the line passes through 10 tunnels, over five viaducts and 11 bridges, while the line between Neral and Lonavla passes through stunning countryside of ravines countryside, the line has gradients of one in 37 to overcome problems posed by 'the big step' the hills presented.

Matheran → *Phone code: 021483. Population: 6000. Altitude: 785 m.*
Mumbai's nearest hill station, in an extension of the Sahyadri Range, Matheran (meaning 'Mother Forest' or 'Wooded Head') has stunning views, refreshingly cool air and pleasant walks. Though very much geared towards the Mumbai weekend crowd, it maintains its unique sense of quiet by banning all forms of motor vehicles within the town. A visit is recommended, but stay a night as it is too strenuous to do in a day from Mumbai. Check road conditions before planning a trip in the monsoons. Limited tourist information is available from the **MTDC Resort** ① *3 km uphill from the centre in Dasturi Naka, T02148-230540.*

The town sprawls out along a north-south ridge and there are splendid views down the almost sheer hillsides to the valleys below. The best views are from Little Chouk, Louisa and Porcupine, which is also known as **Sunset Point**. Allow one hour to walk and see the stunning sunsets. From the northernmost vantage points you can see the lights of Mumbai on a clear night. The layout of the town conforms with standard British Hill Station planning with central civic buildings and dispersed bungalows. You can do your sightseeing on horseback here.

The most scenic route for this diversion is by the spectacular light railway through the ghats from Neral, which is closed during the monsoon. You will appreciate the problems facing the early railway engineers here (see box, page 62). The steam engines are no longer used after working the route for 77 years but you will see one proudly displayed at the station.

Vajreshwari, Akloli and Ganeshpuri
Some 81 km northeast of Mumbai, **Vajreshwari** is renowned for its temple, built by the Maratha warrior Chamiji Appa after hammering the Portuguese at Bassein, but even more so for the **Akloli hot springs**, which pour into an unattractive collection of concrete tanks beside the river Tansa. There are more springs, quieter than those at Akloli, 2 km away in **Ganeshpuri** – locals claim to be able to boil rice in one of the tanks. The village is full of temples, including one to the 20th-century sage Nityanand, who established the nearby **Shri Gurudev Ashram**, a popular destination for foreign seekers.

Around Mumbai listings

For Sleeping and Eating price codes and other relevant information, see pages 14-17.

🛏 Sleeping

Matheran *p64*
Budget hotels near the station can be very noisy. Prices often include meals and rise considerably during holidays (eg Diwali) but most offer good off-season discounts.
$$$$ Usha Ascot, MG Rd, T02148-230360, www.ushaascot.com. 64 rooms, most a/c, pool, sauna, tennis courts, health club, disco.
$$$$-$$$ The Byke, T02148-230365, www.thebyke.com. Good pool, 46 comfortable rooms, 5 a/c, great restaurants (pure vegetarian only).
$$$ Lord's Central, MG Marg, T02148-230228, www.matheranhotels.com. Perched on a ridge with excellent views, 23 colonial-style rooms in 4 bungalows ('Valley' room best), restaurant (meals included), bar, pool, park, riding, friendly. Recommended.
$$ Royal, Kasturba Bhavan, T02148-230247. Health club, 61 rooms, 5 a/c, restaurant, bar.
$$-$ Alexander, Alexander Pt, T02148-230069. In unspoilt woodland, 24 rooms, 3 a/c, good restaurant.
$$-$ Holiday Camp (MTDC), 30 mins uphill from centre 1 km before Matheran (train stops at camp), T02148-230540. 39 rooms cottages, for 2-4, and dorm, limited catering.

$ Girivihar, Shivaji Rd, T02148-230231. Quiet, spacious gardens, some rooms with balconies.
$ Hope Hall, MG Marg (opposite Lord's Central). Good-sized, clean rooms with bath (bucket hot water), friendly family, pleasant location.
$ Prasanna, opposite railway station, T02148-230258. Restaurant, 10 small, clean rooms.

🍴 Eating

Matheran *p64*
$ Kwality Fruit Juice House, MG Rd, south of the train station among many. Excellent honey and *chikki* (a sweet peanut brittle).
$ Woodlands, Chinoy Rd. Indian.

⛰ Activities and tours

Elephanta Caves *p60*
MTDC, T022-2284 5678, launches with good guides leave the Gateway of India every 30 mins 0900-1500 (last one leaves Elephanta at 1730) except during the monsoon (Jun-Sep). The pleasant journey takes 1-1½ hrs Rs 80-100 return). The higher fare is for 'deluxe' boats with an open upper deck. However, the boat boys demand extra payment to sit on top! Small private boats without guides continue during the monsoon when the seas can be very rough.

Kanheri Caves *p63*

MTDC tours from Mumbai; or by train to
Borivli station (from Mumbai Central, 30 mins).
From there, by taxi or auto-rickshaw (10 km),
or by bus on Sun and public holidays.

⊖ Transport

Chaul, Kihim and Alibag beaches *p62*
From the **New Ferry Wharf** at the Gateway
of India in Mumbai, it is a 90-min trip to
Mandwa (Rs 60-110) then a 6-km bus or auto
ride to **Kihim**; or 30-km bus ride to **Chaul**.

Bassein (Vasai) *p63*

Trains go from **Mumbai Central** to Vasai Rd
station, then hire a taxi for 11 km.

Matheran *p64*

From Neral, south of Kalyan, the narrow
gauge train takes 2 hrs to cover the 21 km to
Matheran. The station is in the town centre.
A tax (Rs 25) is charged on arrival (pay before
leaving the station). It's best to book in
advance; essential on weekends. Sit on the
right on the way up for the best views; 1st
class window seats are Nos 1, 4, 5, 8. From
Neral, trains depart daily at 0730, 0850, 1015,
1135 and 1705 (also 1410 on weekends).
From **Matheran**, depart 0700, 0945, 1340,
1445, 1625 (also 1740 on weekends). To
reach Neral from Mumbai CST, take a Pune-
bound express train to **Karjat**, and backtrack
on one of the regular local trains, or a 'fast'
local train direct to Neral. The *Deccan Exp
11007* at 0710; *Koyna Exp 17307* at 0845.
From **Pune** *Sahyadri Exp* at 0730. Taxis to
Matheran can go no further than the MTDC
Resort in Dasturi Naka, from where you can
walk (porters available for luggage) or take
a hand-pulled rickshaw.

❶ Directory

Matheran *p64*

Post office and tourist office opposite railway
station. **Union Bank of India**, MG Rd, changes
TCs and cash, poor rate; also **Hotel Prasanna**.

Around Ahmedabad

Architecture buffs will find much to occupy them around the capital, from Modhera's ancient Sun Temple and the fabulous step well in Patan to the more modern, esoteric charms of Le Corbusier's Gandhinagar. The hills that rise up toward the Rajasthan border hide a number of wildlife sanctuaries and small palace hotels, while a side trip to the south could take in the Nalsarovar Bird Sanctuary and the desolate remains of Lothal, one of the world's oldest ports.

North of Ahmedabad → *For listings, see pages 86-87.*

The fertile irrigated land immediately north of Ahmedabad becomes increasingly arid towards Rajasthan. When approaching Mehsana there are signs of the growing economy, including natural gas, fertilizers, milk products and rapeseed oil processing. There are some worthy trips in this area.

Gandhinagar → *Phone code: 02712 or 082 from Ahmedabad. Population: 195,900.*

When Bombay state was divided along linguistic lines into Maharashtra and Gujarat in 1960, a new capital city was planned for Gujarat named after Mahatma Gandhi. As with Chandigarh, Le Corbusier was instrumental in the design. The 30 residential sectors around the central government complex are similarly impersonal. Construction began in 1965 and the Secretariat was completed in 1970. Located 23 km north of Ahmedabad, Gandhinagar – with multiplex theatre complexes and parks – has become a popular place for day-trippers from Ahmedabad.

Akshardham ① *Sector 20, Nov-Feb 0900-1830, Mar-Oct 1000-2000, part closed on Mon, Rs 25, no cameras or electronic devices*, is a temple with a cultural complex and entertainment park and is run by volunteers. Though not on the same scale as its counterpart in Delhi, the pink sandstone main building, floodlit at dusk, exhibits similar architectural influences. It houses a 2-m-high gold leaf idol and some relics of Sri Swaminarayan, who established the headquarters of his 19th-century Vedic revivalist movement in the Gujarati town of Loj. The three exhibition halls feature a variety of informative sound and light presentations relating to Sri Swaminarayan, the *Vedas* and the Hindu epics. Sahajanabad Vun, the garden for meditation, is impressive and has 'singing fountains' and a restaurant.

Mehsana (Mahesana)

Mehsana, 80 km north of Ahmedabad, has an impressive Jain temple, built in the 1980s in traditional architectural style. Mehsana is used by visitors to Modhera and Patan for an overnight stop. Women travellers have reported being hassled by men near the bus station.

Modhera

ⓘ *Sunrise-sunset, foreigners Rs 100, video camera Rs 25. A Classical Dance Festival is held on the 3rd weekend in Jan.*

Virtually a deserted hamlet 25 km west of Mehsana, Modhera has the remains of one of the finest Hindu temples in Gujarat. Quite off the beaten track, it retains a great deal of its atmosphere and charm. Visit early in the day as it get busy. The partially ruined **Surya** (Sun) **Temple** (1026), built during the reign of Bhimdev I and consecrated in 1026-1027, two centuries before the Sun Temple at Konark, is a product of the great Solanki period (eighth to 13th centuries). Despite the temple's partial destruction by subsequent earthquakes that may have accounted for the collapse of its tower, it remains an outstanding monument, set against the backdrop of a barren landscape. Superb carvings of goddesses, birds, beasts and blossoms decorate the remaining pillars. Over the last 20 years the complex has undergone major restoration by the Archaeological Survey of India, which is continuing as funds permit. Unlike the temple at Konark, the main temple stands well above the surrounding land, raised by a high brick terrace faced with stone.

A rectangular *kund* (pool), now dry, over 50 m long and 20 m wide, with flights of steps and subsidiary shrines, faces the front of the temple. A remarkable structure, despite the damage caused by weathering, it is still possible to gain an impression of the excellence of the carving. On the west side of the tank a steep flight of steps leads up to the main entrance of the east *mandapa* through a beautifully carved *torana*, of which only the pillars now remain. The **sabha mandapa**, a pillared hall, is 15 sq m. Note the cusped arches which became such a striking feature of Mughal buildings 600 years later. The corbelled roof of this entry hall, which has been reconstructed, is a low stepped pyramid. Beautiful columns and magnificent carvings decorate the hall. The western part of the oblong temple contains the raised **inner sanctuary**. The upper storeys have been completely destroyed, though it clearly consisted of a low pyramidal roof in front of the tall *sikhara* (tower) over the sanctuary itself. Surya's image in the sanctuary (now missing) was once illuminated by the first rays of the rising sun at each solar equinox (proof of the mathematical and astronomical knowledge of the designers). Images of Surya and Agni are among the more well-preserved carvings on the external walls which also contain some erotic scenes. The interior walls were plain other than for niches to house images of Surya.

Patan

Little visited, Patan has more than 100 beautifully carved Jain temples and many attractive traditionally carved wooden houses. It remains a centre for fine textiles, particularly silk *patola* saris produced by the characteristic *ikat* technique which involves tie-dyeing the warp threads before weaving to create designs on the finished fabrics. Only three extended families (at Salvivad and Fatipal Gate) can be seen at work on the highly prized double *ikat* weaving where both the warp and the weft threads are tie-dyed before being set on traditional looms – only to be found in Indonesia and Japan outside India. It takes three to six months to weave a sari, hence each piece sells for at least Rs 120,000; samples are Rs 2000. You can see them in production at the Salvi brothers' **workshop** ⓘ *Patolawala St, T02766-232274, www.patanpatola.com.* Patan is 35 km northwest of Mehsana and can be reached either by bus or train. Buses also run from Modhera.

The spectacular **Rani ki Vav** (11th century) ⓘ *sunrise-sunset, Rs 100 foreigners; video camera Rs 25, 4 km from Patan Bus Stand,* named after a Solanki queen, is one of the largest step wells in India with superb carvings on seven storeys. Flights of steps lead down to the water, lined by string courses of sculptured voluptuous women, Vishnu avatars and goddesses. The **Sahasralinga Talao**, 4.5 km from Patan Bus Stand, is a cluster of Solanki period (11th-12th century) shrines facing a small lake. Excavations are in progress.

Vadnagar

The town, 40 km northeast of Mehsana, has the finest example of the *torana* arches that characterize North Gujarat. Beautiful sculptures decorate two of the original four 12th-century arched gateways on *kirti stambha* pillars. The Solanki period city gates are beautifully sculpted, the best being near the lake. The impressive 17th-century **Haktesvar temple**, the most important Siva temple in Gujarat, has fine carvings, erotic sculpture and a silver shrine. Tana-Riri, two poetess-singers from Vadnagar, are said to have saved Tansen from the burning effects of the *Deepak Raga* (Song of Fire) by singing the *Maldaar Raga* (Song of Rain). Akbar invited the sisters to sing in his court, but rather than refuse to sing for a Muslim emperor (which was against their custom) they immolated themselves. Their shrine can be seen at Vadnagar.

Taranga

Named after Tara Devi, Taranga, 55 km northeast of Mehsana by bus, has a wonderful complex of well-preserved, if somewhat over-restored, 12th-century Jain temples surrounded by spectacular hills. The large central sandstone temple to Adinatha is beautifully carved with sensual dancing figures, Hindu deities and Jain *Tirthankaras*. Inside is a bejewelled central statue carved out of a single piece of alabaster. There is a scenic trek from the main Adinath temple, passing some dramatic rock formations, to the hilltop Shilp Temple where one of the Jain saints meditated. Panthers have been sighted near the temple complex.

Ambaji

Close to the Rajasthan border, en route to Mount Abu, Ambaji is known for its marble mines. You can see marble artisans at work at this temple town (and at Khedbrahma nearby) where **Bhadra Purnima fair** is held, with processions of flag bearing pilgrims followed by musicians and dancers. A picturesque ropeway goes to Gabbar hill, a holy pilgrimage for Hindus (Rs 40). Ahmedabad–Mount Abu buses stop at Ambaji.

The five 11th- and 12th-century Jain temples just east of Ambaji at **Kumbhariya** ① *0630-1930, Aarti worship 0900-0930 and 1900, tea canteen, very cheap thalis*, are worth visiting for their exquisite marble carvings. Be sure to see the second temple; the main one has been largely rebuilt. Catch a jeep from Ambaji Bus Stand.

Danta

En route from Taranga to Ambaji, the princely state of Danta was known for its cavalry. It is dominated by the medieval **Parmara Rajput Fort**. The jungles and rocky hills harbour panther, nilgai and four-horned antelope, and there is extensive birdlife. To explore, bicycles can be hired from in the village.

Poshina

The small 15th-century Poshina Fort, 45 km south of Abu Road, stands at the confluence of two holy rivers (Sai and Panhari) with views over the hills. It was the capital of the North

Gujarat branch of Vaghela Rajputs. There are ancient Jain and Siva temples nearby as well as tribal villages where you can watch arrow making, potters, basketwork and silversmiths. You will find collections of up to 2000 terracotta horses here – the story goes that you make a wish and then if that wish comes true, you make an offering of one or many horses (depending on the size of the wish) and a *puja*. It's quite magical. The area is home to Bhils, colourful Garasias and Rabaris who herd camels, cattle and goats. The busy and interesting **market** centre is well worth stopping at; the last stretch of the approach road is very poor. Ahmedabad–Ambaji buses stop at Kheroj from where it is possible to get shared jeeps to Poshina (12 km).

Chitra Vichitra Fair is held a fortnight after **Holi** at **Gunbakhari**, 8 km away. It is attended by Bhils, Garasias and Rabaris (some of whom are now abandoning their traditional *dhotis* and turbans). The fair is very colourful with much revelry, dancing and singing, food stalls etc. Matchmaking is often followed by elopements. **Florican Tours** ① *T079-2550 6590*, can arrange visits to the fair. Try staying in a tent (contact **Gujarat Tourism**) during the fair. Delicious flavoured *lassi* is available near the village entrance but ask for it be prepared with your own filtered or mineral water.

Vijaynagar

Stunning ruined Hindu and Jain temples hide away in an enchanting forest in Vijaynagar. Once part of a kingdom ruled by the Rathod Rajputs of Marwar, Vijaynagar is home to a beautiful groups of temples. In some places, it feels as if the forest has won as it grows through the temples, but a lot of work has gone into clearing the areas around the temples and there are even paved pathways and signboards. It's incredibly atmospheric, especially late afternoon. There is one Shiva temple still active within the forest, which is quite magical.

Palanpur and Balaram

The *maqbara* with fine mausolea in the old Nawabi capital of Palanpur stands rather neglected. The palace is now the court; look in to see the fabulous ceiling paintings and sandalwood carvings. The 1915 Kirti Stambha has the 700-year-long history of the Nawabs of Palanpur inscribed on it. Nearby Balaram has one of the best-kept palace hotels in Gujarat (see page 86), 3 km off the highway and 14 km north of Palanpur. About 20 km from there, the **Jessore Bear Sanctuary** in the Aravallis has sloth bear (occasionally spotted), panther, nilgai, sambhar, four-horned antelope, etc, but these are best seen by climbing Jessore hill.

South of Ahmedabad → *For listings, see pages 86-87.*

Vautha

The **Vautha Mela**, starting at Kartik Purnima (November), is held at the confluence of the Sabarmati and Vatrak rivers, some 46 km south of Ahmedabad. Less colourful than Pushkar fair it is also far less touristy. About 4000 donkeys, painted in vivid colours, and over 2000 camels are traded. There is a great atmosphere on the river banks early in the morning, with haggling over animals and craft sales. **Gujarat Tourism** provides tents and catering.

Nalsarovar Bird Sanctuary

The sanctuary, 65 km southwest of Ahmedabad, is noted for waterbirds including migratory ducks, flamingos and geese. The lake and the Surendranagar Reservoirs were declared a bird sanctuary in 1969. Uniquely in Saurashtra, Nalsarovar is surrounded by reed beds and marshes though the lake often dries out before the rains. Bharwad and Jat herdsmen and their water buffaloes live on the reed islands; you can get hot buttered millet chapatis and chutney with sweet tea or *lassi* from some shacks. Padhar fisherfolk who live around the lake are good artisans. **Forest Department Bungalows** have two or three simple rooms and views of lake. The best time to visit is November to February.

Lothal 'Mound of the dead'

① *Sat-Thu 1000-1700, Rs 100 for foreigners. There's no shade or proper drinks outlet so carry bottled water.*

Southeast of Moenjodaro, 720 km as the crow flies, Lothal has some of the most substantial remains of the Harappan culture in India dating from circa 2500-1700 BC. Once a port sandwiched between the Sabarmati River and the Bhogavo River, it is now 10 km inland from the Gulf of Khambhat on a flat, often desolate-looking plain. Thorn scrub and parched soils surround the site and even in February a hot desiccating wind picks up flurries of dust. Lothal's location and function as a port have led most authorities to argue that it was settled by Harappan trading communities who came by sea from the mouths of the Indus. Others suggest that the traders came by an overland route. The site is surrounded by a mud-brick embankment 300 m north–south and 400 m east–west. Unlike the defensive walls at Harappa and Moenjodaro, the wall at Lothal enclosed the workers' area as well as the citadel. The presence of a dry dock and a warehouse further distinguish it from other major Harappan sites. Some visitors find that the recent restoration work has made the walls look too modern.

The massive excavated **dry dock** runs along the east wall of the city. A 12-m-wide gap in the north side is believed to have been the entrance by which boats came into the dock, while a spillway over the south wall allowed excess water to overflow. The city wall at this point may have been a wharf for unloading. Excavations of the warehouse suggest that trade was the basis of Lothal's existence. The building at the southwest corner of the wharf had a high platform made of cubical mud-brick blocks, the gaps between them allowing ventilation. Over 65 Indus Valley seals discovered here show pictures of packing material, bamboo or rope, suggestive of trade; one from Bahrain is evidence of overseas trade. Excavations show a **planned city** in a grid pattern, with an underground drainage system, wells and brick houses with baths and fireplaces. The raised brick platform to the southeast may have been a kiln where seals and plaques were baked. Objects found include painted pottery, terracotta toys, ivory, shell, semi-precious stone items, bangles and necklaces made of tiny gold beads. Rice and millet were clearly in use, and there is evidence that horses had been domesticated. The nearby cemetery had large funerary vessels indicating pit burials.

Wadhwan

Northwest of Limbdi, Wadhwan was a princely state of the Jhalas, a Rajput clan. The fortified old township has plenty of interesting architecture including two old step wells with attractive carvings and some fine 11th- to 16th-century temples. It is an ideal place to watch and shop for *bandhani*, wood and stone carving, silverwork and textiles.

The opulent 19th-century **Raj Mahal** (*Bal Vilas*) occupied by the royal family has a grand Durbar hall with chandeliers, frescoes, carved furniture, crystal and velvet curtains, Sheesh Mahal library and billiard room. The vast landscaped gardens contain lily ponds and fountains. Maharajah Chaitanya Dev is a keen restorer of classic cars and has a vintage car collection.

Around Ahmedabad listings

For Sleeping and Eating price codes and other relevant information, see pages 14-17.

⊙ Sleeping

Gandhinagar *p81*

$$$-$$ Fortune Inn Haveli, Sector 11, opposite Sachivalaya, T079-3988 4422, www.fortunehotels.in. 84 below-par rooms, restaurants, exchange, car hire, free airport transfer, Wi-Fi.

$ Youth Hostel, Sector 16, T079-2322 2364. 2 rooms, 42 beds in 6-bed and 8-bed dorms, very good, no reservations.

Mehsana *p81*

$$$-$$ Water World Resort, 25 mins' drive out of town, T02762-282351, www.waterworldresort.com. A/c cottages, modern, Mughal garden with a/c 'royal tents', vegetarian restaurant, wave pool, sports complex, lake.

$ Natraj, 1 km from bus stand. 12 rooms (dorms to a/c with bath), good veggie restaurant.

$ Railway Retiring Rooms. (Rs 70) with bath.

Patan *p82*

$ Surya Palace, University Rd, near railway crossing, T02766-329872. Cheap and cheerful, not very inspiring, but quieter than Yuvraj.

$ Toran Tourist Bungalow, Gujarat Tourism. 2 simple rooms, café, convenient for step well.

$ Yuvraj, opposite bus stand, T02766-281397. Wide range of rooms, some a/c, convenient but noisy location, restaurant serves very cheap unlimited *thalis*.

Danta *p83*

$$ Bhavani Villa, on a hilltop, T02749-278705, www.bhavanivilladanta.com. Very welcoming. 4 modern a/c rooms facing the hills, 1 non-a/c in colonial period mansion, delicious Rajput meals, friendly hosts – it's like staying with family, great for nature lovers, game drives, riding (Rs 400 per hr), very good horse safaris (Rs 5000 per person). Get a tour of their farm – lovely scenery. Recommended.

Poshina *p83*

$$$ Darbargadh (Heritage Hotel), fort complex, www.poshina.com. Reservations: Florican Tours, T079-2550 6590. In 17th-century wing of the fort. Pleasant with open courtyards and hill views, old world charm, now renovated with antiques, Rajasthani miniatures and rare Tanjore paintings, 15 comfortable, air-cooled rooms , spicy Indian meals, camel rides, friendly owner is knowledgeable about local tribes and crafts, good village safaris, folk entertainment. Your host is the Secretary of the Heritage Hotels Association Gujarat. Recommended.

Vijaynagar *p84*

$$$ Vijay Villas (Heritage Hotel), T07926 747690, www.vijayvilasvijaynagar.com. Home away from home in this heritage-style property. Nice rooms around little courtyard and great family food on offer. Beautifully located near polo forest.

Balaram *p84*

$$ Balaram Palace Resort, Chitrasani, T079-2657 6388, www.balarampalace.com. Splendid riverside location surrounded by hills but little bit soulless. Well-restored 1930s palace, 17 a/c rooms (interiors too modern

Rs 100, with a sculpted façade, pretty jharoka windows and carved stone pillars, has an impressive Darbar Hall and a museum of paintings, furniture, brass and silver. Silver items include caskets, models of buildings and scales used for weighing the Maharajah (he was weighed against silver and gold on his 25th and 50th birthday; the precious metals were then distributed to the poor). A gallery has toys from the 1930s and 1940s. The **Vintage and Classic Car Museum** ① *open same hours, Rs 100,* is one of the finest in the country. Exhibits include 1910 New Engine, 1920s Delage and Daimler, 1935-1955 models, horse-drawn carriages, etc. Boating is possible on **Veri Lake** nearby, which attracts large numbers of rosy pelicans, flamingos, demoiselle and common eastern cranes and many others, particularly in January and February. You can visit the **Bhuvaneshwari Ayurvedic Pharmacy**, founded in 1910, which still prepares herbal medicines according to ancient principles and runs a hospital offering massages and treatment. The early 20th-century **Swaminarayan Temple** has painted interiors on the upper floors.

Rajkot

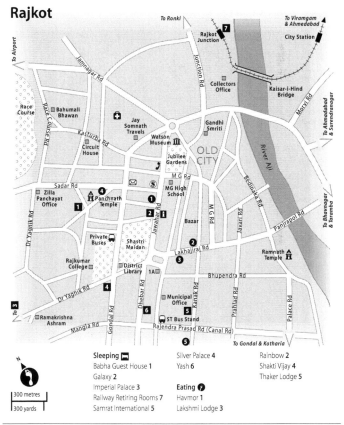

Sleeping 🛏
Babha Guest House 1
Galaxy 2
Imperial Palace 3
Railway Retiring Rooms 7
Samrat International 5

Silver Palace 4
Yash 6

Eating 🍴
Havmor 1
Lakshmi Lodge 3

Rainbow 2
Shakti Vijay 4
Thaker Lodge 5

Wankaner

On a bend of the Machchu River, Wankaner (*wanka* – curve, *ner* – river), another capital of the Jhala Rajputs, was founded in 1605. The old ruler, Amar Sinhji, was known for his flamboyant lifestyle but also introduced wide-ranging reforms in farmers' co-operatives, education, roads, tramways and internal security. He was also responsible for building the **Ranjitvilas Palace** (1907 extension to the 1880s British Residents' bungalow), visible for miles across the plains. It is built in a strange mix of styles (Venetian façades, a Dutch roof, *jarokha* balconies, a 'Mughal' pavilion, minarets, English clock tower, etc) yet all is very well integrated. The garage has an interesting collection of models from the 1930s and 1940s and a 1921 Silver Ghost, jeeps, wagons and old buggies, while there are Kathiawadi horses in the stables. A part of the palace is now a **museum** brim full of royal memorabilia of a bygone lifestyle. There is an interesting step well with marble balustrade staircases, cool, subterranean chambers and marble statues of Vishnu.

Dhrangadhra

The pretty little village town of Dhrangadhra is the government Forest Department's headquarters for the **Little Rann of Kachchh Wild Ass Sanctuary** ① *T02754-223016*. It was also the capital of a very progressive princely state, which had English and vernacular schools in 1855 and free education in the early 1900s. Full-day jeep tours of Little Rann, to see wild asses, salt mining communities and a bird sanctuary, cost Rs 2000 for two, including a delicious home-cooked lunch.

Bhavnagar and around → *For listings, see pages 117-128. Phone code: 0278.*
Population: 511,000.

Bhavnagar was ruled by progressive rulers from its foundation in 1723. Surrounded by flat and richly cultivated land, it is now a major industrial town and cotton export centre, and is rapidly becoming one of India's most important ship-building ports. However, most of its character is preserved in the bazars of the Old City where you can pick your way through the crowded lanes amongst the old merchants' *havelis*.

The palace-like **Takhtsinghji Hospital** (1879-1883) was designed by Sir William Emerson. The 18th-century **Darbargadh** (Old Palace, extended 1894-1895), in the town centre, now houses the State Bank but is scarcely visible in the incredibly overcrowded and dirty Darbargadh Bazar. **Barton Museum** (1895) ① *0900-1300, 1400-1800, Rs 5*, in an impressive crescent-shaped building, has a collection of coins, carvings, geological and archaeological finds, farming implements, arms and armour, handicrafts, miniature paintings and excellent bead and silk embroidery. The better known **Gandhi Smriti** ① *0830-1230, 1500-1900, free*, is dedicated to Mahatma Gandhi (he was at university here; his old college is now an Ayurvedic education centre). Photos portray his life and the freedom struggle. There are also letters and mark sheets showing his scores at university. The unremarkable marble **Takhteshwar Temple** on a hillock has good views over the city and the distant coastline.

Victoria Park, 2 km from the centre, is a former royal hunting preserve. Far removed from the image conveyed by its name of a manicured British city park, it has rolling scrub forests and marshes rich in birdlife. Nilgai, hyena, jackal, jungle cat and monitor lizard can all be seen. A pleasant stroll from the **Nilambagh Palace**, it is a great place for walks.

Gaurishankar Lake, a popular escape from the city with parks and steps along the embankments, is good for winter birdwatching when cranes, pelicans and ducks arrive. Plovers, terns and other birds nest on the islands.

Velavadar National Park

① *Some 10 km off the Bhavnagar–Vadodara Highway, 0630-0830 and 1630-1830, closed mid-Jun to mid-Oct, US$5, camera US$5; guide (some don't speak English), US$10 per trip, jeep US$25 per drive. Pay at Forest Range Office at park entrance.*

The compact 36 sq km of flat grassland broken by dry open scrubland and patches of thorn forest was set up to protect the Indian blackbuck, of which it has the largest population in the country – about 1000 permanent residents and another 1000 that wander in from the surrounding area. The Bhavnagar royal family came here for cheetah coursing, falconry and hunting and also harvested grass for fodder for their cattle and horses.

The blackbuck is the second largest of the antelopes and the fastest long-distance runner of all animals. It can keep going at a steady 90 kph. The black-and-white dominant males sport spiral horns; the juvenile males are brown and white while the hornless females are brownish, with lighter parts. It is one of the most hunted animals in India, and

Bhavnagar

To New Port
Creek
OLD CITY
To Velavadar
Station Rd
Mahatma Gandhi Rd
To Port Office
Bike Hire
BAZAR
AMBA CHOWK
S 7
DARBARGADH
Ganga Devi
IAC
High Court Rd
High Court
To Victoria Park, Gaurishankar Lake & Ahmedabad
To Sihor
Town Hall
Taxis
Panwadi Chowk
Pill Gardens
6
ST Station Rd
Galaxy Cinema
Punjab Travels
Barton Museum & Gandhi Smriti
Clock Tower
4 5
Forest Office
ST Bus Stand
NEW TOWN
ATM S
2
Tanna Travels
Waghawadi Rd
ATM S
Diamond Chowk
Takhtsinghji Hospital
Takhteshwar Temple
To University & Diu
To Talaja
To Airport

N
500 metres
500 yards

so is an endangered species. Impressive males clash horns to establish territory and court females. Wolves, their prime predator, have been reduced to only two families, but they can still be seen. The park also contains a few sounders of wild boar in addition to 50-60 nilgai, usually seen near waterholes, jungle cat, which can be seen at dawn and dusk, and jackal. Birdlife is rich with numerous birds of prey including the largest harrier roost in the world; some 1500 to 2000 of these light-bodied hawks gather here at sunset in November and December. During the monsoon the park is the best place in India to spot the lesser florican. In addition to the two rivers that border the park, there are three waterholes and three small pools that attract animals at midday.

Sihor

Midway between Bhavnagar (27 km) and Palitana, the former Gohil Rajput capital has the 17th-century hilltop **Darbargadh Palace** (now government offices). Though rather dilapidated, you can still see some intricate carved wooden balconies and pillars outside and 19th-century wall paintings inside. The Brahm **Kund** (11th-12th century), about 2 km west of Sihor centre and 500 m south of the main road, is a deeply set stepped tank (now empty). It has around 100 sculpted images of deities in small niches, a few of which are still actively worshipped. There are also pillared galleries with rich carvings of musicians. In the village nearby brass utensils are produced as a cottage industry by rolling scrap from the Alang ship breaking yard and beating it into attractive water pots. Villagers are only too happy to show you around their workshops. The **Khodiyar Temple** on the Bhavnagar–Sihor road is in a pretty setting among the hills.

Palitana → *For listings, see pages 117-128. Phone code: 02848. Population: 51,900. Area: 13 sq km.*

Palitana is renowned for the extraordinary Jain temple complex on Shatrunjaya Hill which attracts domestic pilgrims as well as foreign visitors. No one is allowed to remain on the hill at night, but even during the day there is a peaceful serenity as you listen to the temple bells and pilgrims chanting in the City of the Gods. Information is available from the **tourist office** ① *Hotel Toran Sumeru, T02848-252327.*

Background

Palitana was the capital of a small princely state founded by Shahji, a Gohel Rajput who belonged to the same clan as the Maharajah of Bhavnagar. The river Khari bisects the town. The east bank has hotels, eateries, shopping centres and bus and railway stations, while the west bank has the Willingdon Vegetable Market and some older raj and royal buildings. The last ruler died leaving wives and sisters to fight over the royal palace and mansions that are now decaying but show signs of impressive architecture. The better houses are on Taleti Road. The busy little town is also known for diamond cutting and horse breeding. South African diamonds are imported from Belgium for cutting and polishing before being re-exported back to Belgium.

Temple complex

① *Shatrunjaya Hill, 3 km southwest of Palitana, 0700-1900, free, camera Rs 40, visitors should wear clean respectable clothes, leather articles (even watch straps) and food or drink are not allowed in the temple area, but can be left, along with shoes, at the entrance. Take lots of water and a sun hat, arrive by dawn to join the pilgrims, and allow 2 hrs for the climb, 4-5 hrs for the round trip. You can be carried up by a dhooli (string chair – Rs 500 return) but the hassle from aggressive touts in the early stages of the climb can be substantial (rates rise in summer, peaking during fairs and Mahavir Jayanti to Rs 1000).*

According to local tradition, Adinatha, the first Tirthankara, visited the hill several times and the first temple was erected by his son. Thereafter, the temple builders could not stop. Jains believe that Pundarika, the chief disciple of Adinatha, attained Nirvana here.

Most of the temples are named after their founders and date from the 16th century, although the earliest may date from the 11th. It would appear that many others were destroyed by the Muslims in the 14th and 15th centuries, but later, when Jains obtained religious toleration, they began rebuilding.

The 863 temples are strung along the two ridges of the hill, with further temples in the hollow between, linking them. There are nine enclosures of *tuks* (fortifications) which provided defence. There are lovely views over the flat, cultivated black soils of the coastal plain, and on a clear day after the rains it is sometimes possible to see the Gulf of Khambat away to the east, and the Chamardi Peak and the granite range of Sihor to the north.

There are two routes up the 600-m climb. The main route starts in the town of Palitana to the east of the hill, while a shorter and steeper route climbs up from the village of Adpur to the west. Both are stepped paths in excellent condition. The main pilgrim route starts in Palitana. Over 3500 steps – you will be told more by the *dhoolie* carriers at the bottom – lead up to the temples. There are two long flat stretches, but since some of the path is unshaded, even in winter it can get very hot.

Temples in this southern group include one of **Ramaji Gandharia** (16th century), and the **Bhulavani** (labyrinth, 18th century) which is a series of crypt-like chambers each surmounted with a dome. The **Hathiapol** (Elephant Gate, 19th century) faces southeast. The **Vimalavasi Tuk** occupies the west end of the south ridge. In it is the **Adishvara Temple** (16th century) which dominates the site. It has a double-storey *mandapa* inside which is a large image of Rishabhanatha with crystal eyes and a gold crown of jewels. The **Vallabhai Temple** (19th century) with its finely clustered spires and the large **Motisah Temple** (1836) occupy the middle ground between the ridges.

The **Khartaravasi Tuk** is the largest and highest temple complex, stretched out along the northern Ridge and includes the **Adinatha Temple** (16th century). There are quadruple *Tirthankara* images inside the sanctuary.

A comprehensive restoration project is being carried out on some of the temples, with many of the old stone carvings being 'refreshed' using a butterscotch-coloured mortar. It is interesting to watch the craftsmen in action, but some may feel that the new decorations lack the sculptural finesse and timeworn appeal of the originals.

If you wish to take the track down to Adpur turn left out of the complex entrance courtyard where you leave your shoes. Follow the sign to Gheti Pag Gate.

Coast south of Bhavnagar → *For listings, see pages 117-128.*

Alang

The beach at Alang has turned into the world's largest scrapyard for redundant ships, the industry yielding rich pickings from the sale of salvaged metal (bronze, copper) and the complete range of ship's fittings from portholes to furniture, diesel engines and lifeboats.

Alang village, which is 50 km south of Bhavnagar, has developed this surprising specialization because of the unusual nature of its tides. The twice-monthly high tides are exceptional, reputedly the second highest in the world, lifting ships so that they can be beached well on shore, out of reach of the sea for the next two weeks. During this period the breakers move in unhindered. Labourers' 'huts' line the coast road though many workers commute from Bhavnagar.

Even though entry to Alang port may not be available, the last few kilometres to the port are lined with the yards of dealers specializing in every item of ships' furniture. Valuable items are creamed off before the 'breaking' begins, but if you want 3-cm-thick porthole glass, a spare fridge-freezer or a life jacket, this is the place to browse. However, customs officers always get first choice of valuables as they have to give permission for vessels to be beached, so don't expect too much. Some have found the journey not worth the trouble since they couldn't enter the fenced-off 'lots'.

Alang is only open to tourists with **special permission**, obtained from the **Gujarat Maritime Board** ① *Sector 10A, opposite Air Force Station, Gandhinagar, T02842-235222*, the **Port Officer** ① *New Port, Bhavnagar 5, T0278-229 3090*, or in Alang itself. Foreigners report finding it difficult to get permission to enter the beach/port area. Hotels in Bhavnagar may be able to help individuals gain entry but permits for groups are virtually impossible. Photography is not allowed. Strong shoes and modest dress are recommended.

Mahuva and Gopnath

The picturesque town of **Mahuva** (pronounced Mow-va), south of Palitana, was known for its historic port. Beautiful handcrafted furniture with lacquer work and intricate hand painting is made here.

About 30 km northeast of Mahuva, **Gopnath** is where the 16th-century mystic poet Narsinh Mehta is said to have attained enlightenment. Near the lighthouse is the 1940s summer home of late Maharajah Krishna Kumar Singhji of Bhavnagar, part of which is now a hotel. There are pleasant rocky, white-sand beaches – dangerous for swimming but good for walking – and a 700-year-old temple, 1 km away.

Junagadh and around → *For listings, see pages 117-128. Phone code: 0285. Population: 168,700.*

① *You can tackle the town on foot allowing plenty of time for Uparkot. However, it's best to get an early start on Girnar Hill with the help of a rickshaw (around Rs 50 return).*

The narrow winding lanes and colourful bazars of this small town, entered by imposing gateways, are evocative of earlier centuries. A large rock with 14 Asokan edicts, dating from 250 BC, stands on the way to the temple-studded Girnar Hill, believed to be a pre-Harappan site. But the modern town is marred by ugly new buildings and dirty slums.

Established by the Mauryans in the fourth century BC, from the second to fourth centuries Junagadh was the capital of Gujarat under the Kshattrapa rulers. It is also associated with the Chudasama Rajputs who ruled from Junagadh from AD 875. The fort was expanded in 1472 by Mahmud Beghada and again in 1683 and 1880. Sher Khan Babi, who took on the title of Nawab Bahadur Khan Babi, declared Junagadh an independent state in the 1700s. At the time of Partition the Nawab exercised his legal right to accede to Pakistan but his subjects were predominantly Hindu and after Indian intervention and an imposed plebiscite their will prevailed. The Nawab was exiled along with his 100 dogs.

The old **Uparkot Citadel** ① *0700-1900, Rs 5, plus Rs 100 to visit the Buddhist caves*, on a small plateau east of the town, was a stronghold in the Mauryan and Gupta empires. The present walls are said to date from the time of the Chudasama Rajputs (ninth-15th century). The deep moat inside the walls is believed to have once held crocodiles. The Ottoman canons of Suleman Pasha, an ally of the sultans, were moved here after the Muslim forces were unable to save Diu from Portuguese naval forces. The town was repeatedly under attack so there was a huge granary to withstand a long siege. The **Jama Masjid** was built from the remains of a Hindu palace. The 11th-century **Adi Chadi Vav**, a *baoli* with 172 steps and an impressive spiral staircase, is believed to commemorate two slave girls who were bricked up as sacrifice to ensure the supply of water. The 52-m-deep Naghan Kuva is a huge 11th-century well, which has steps down to the water level through the rocks, with openings to ventilate the path. The **Buddhist cave monastery** in

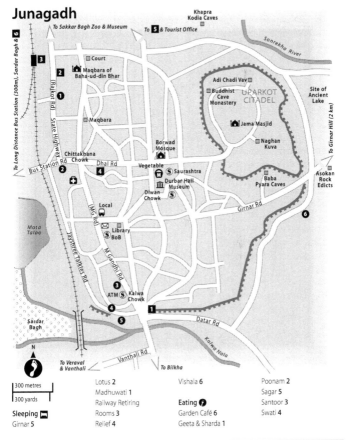

Junagadh

Sleeping 🛏
Girnar 5

Lotus 2
Madhuwati 1
Railway Retiring
Rooms 3
Relief 4

Vishala 6

Eating 🍴
Garden Café 6
Geeta & Sharda 1

Poonam 2
Sagar 5
Santoor 3
Swati 4

this fort complex dates from Asoka's time. Two of the three levels are open to visitors. The drainage system was very advanced, as shown by the rainwater reservoir. The ventilation cleverly achieved a balance of light and cool breezes. Other Buddhist caves are hewn into the hillsides near the fort.

In the town, the late 19th-century mausolea of the Junagadh rulers, not far from the railway station, are impressive. The **Maqbara** of Baha-ud-din Bhar with its silver doors and intricate, elaborate decoration, has an almost fairground flamboyance. The **Old Mausolea** at Chittakhana Chowk (opposite **Relief Hotel**, which has views of them from the roof), which were once impressive, are now crumbling and overgrown.

The **Durbar Hall Museum** ① *Nawab's Palace, circa 1870, Janta Chowk, Thu-Tue 0900-1215, 1500-1800, Rs 5, plus Rs 2 per photo, small but recommended*, houses royal memorabilia, including portraits, palanquins, gem-studded carpets and costumes.

Further east, **Asokan rock edicts** ① *at the foot of the Girnar Hill, 0830-1800, closed Wed and holidays, Rs 100*, are carved in the Brahmi script on a large boulder. The emperor instructed his people to be gentle with women, be kind to animals, give alms freely and to plant medicinal herbs. The 13 edicts are summed up in the 14th.

Girnar Hill, rising 900 m above the surrounding plain, 3 km east of town, has been an important religious centre for the Jains from the third century BC. The climb up this worn volcanic cone by 10,000 stone steps takes at least two hours. You start just beyond Damodar Kund in teak forest; at the foot is the Asokan Edict while a group of 16 Jain temples surmounts the hill. The climb can be trying in the heat so is best started very early in the morning. You will find tea stalls en route and brazen monkeys. *Dhoolis* are available but are expensive. The charge depends on weight; for example, Rs 1500 for 60 kg to the first group of temples, which are the most interesting. There are good views from the top though the air is often hazy.

Sasan Gir National Park → *Phone code: 02877.*

① *0700-1200, 1500 to sunset from mid-Oct to mid-Feb (permits issued 0630-1030 and 1500-1700); 0700-1200, 1600 to sunset mid-Feb to mid-Jun (permits 0630-1100, 1600-1730); best season is Mar-May. Entry permits can be arranged by some hotels, or applied for in advance (ie for 0700 safari apply the previous day) at Sinh Sadan Lodge in Sasan village. Entry fees: US$40 for permit, allowing 6 people in jeep to enter park. New rule is that you have to go in person and show passport, even if your safari is pre-booked with hotel. Additional charge of Rs 500 if your camera exceeds 7.1 megapixels. Count in an extra Rs 100 for a guide and tips (some have little English but can make excellent wildlife spotters). Indians pay roughly 10-25% of foreigner fee. Jeep hire is around Rs 750, but expect all fees, including jeep hire to increase 25% on Sat-Sun and 50% during Navratri, Diwali and Christmas/New Year. Hotel jeeps cost more but may come with English-speaking drivers. Advance bookings recommended as a maximum of 35 jeeps are permitted in the sanctuary at one time, distributed over 6 different routes of 22-50 km. But a few jeeps are available on the day – first come, first shove. Temperature: 42-7°C. Rainfall: 1000 mm.*

The sanctuary covers a total area of 1412 sq km, of which 258 sq km at the core is the national park. As a result of over-grazing and agricultural colonization, only about 10% of the park is forest. However, the scrubby look of much of the area represents the original, natural vegetation. The area has rocky hills and deep valleys with numerous rivers and streams, and there are extensive clearings covered with savannah-like fodder grasses.

The **Asiatic lion** once had a wide range of natural territory running from North to West India through Persia to Arabia. It is now only found in the Gir forest; the last one seen outside India was in 1942, in Iran. Similar to its African cousin, the tawnier Asian is a little smaller and stockier in build with a skin fold on the belly, a thinner mane and a thicker tuft at the end of its tail. The 1913 census accounted for only 18 in the park. The lions' natural habitat was threatened by the gradual conversion of the forest into agricultural land and cattle herders grazing their livestock here. The conservation programme has been remarkably successful. There are now reckoned to be around 350 lions in the park; too many, some say, for the territory to support. These, and 300-plus **panthers**, make Gir arguably India's best big cat sanctuary, while the existence of a handful of Sudanese villages in the park add to the slightly surreal African-safari feel of the place.

Though there have been attacks on villagers by park lions, these are thought likely to have been provoked as there are few reported man-eaters. Nevertheless, relations between the lions and the human settlements within and around the boundaries are becoming increasingly strained, with several reports of revenge killings of lions (principally for hunting livestock) being reported in the last couple of years. Deaths by poaching are also beginning to occur with disturbing regularity.

During the course of three to four jeep safaris you have a reasonably good chance of spotting lions. They are more likely to be seen with the help of a good tracker and guide, but the government system for apportioning guides to a different group each session means it is impossible to guarantee the quality of your tracker from one drive to the next; inevitably, some visitors return disappointed. If you don't see one, the Interpretation Zone's safari park has a few lions (see below).

A **watch tower** camouflaged in the tree canopy at Kamleshwar overlooks an artificial reservoir harbouring wild crocodiles but it is poorly located and overcrowded with bus loads of noisy visitors at weekends. Other towers are at Janwdla and Gola. For birdwatching, Adhodiya, Valadara, Ratnaghuna and Pataliyala, are good spots. A walk along Hiran River is also rewarding.

The Tulsishyam **hot springs** in the heart of the forest (Tulsishyam is also a Krishna pilgrimage centre), and Kankai Mata **temple** dedicated to Bhim, the *Mahabharata* hero, and his mother Kunti, add interest.

Gir Interpretation Zone ① *Devaliya, 12 km west of Sasan, foreigners US$20, Indians Rs 75 for 45-min tour by electric minibus; a taxi will charge around Rs 200-300 return including wait,* is 16 sq km of Gir habitat fenced in as a safari park to show a cross section of wildlife; the four or five lions can be easily seen in open scrubland in the area. The lions here are less shy than those in the sanctuary, but you may be frustrated by the briefness of the encounter. Other Gir wildlife include spotted deer, sambar, nilgai, peafowl. Permits are available at the reception.

Crocodile Rearing Centre ① *near entrance to Sinh Sadan, and road leading to Lion Safari Lodge, 0800-1200, 1500-1800, free,* is full of marsh crocodiles, varying in size from a few centimetres to 1 m, for restocking the population in the sanctuary. Eggs are collected in the park and taken to Junagadh for hatching under controlled conditions. Unfortunately, keepers prod the crocodiles to make them move.

Veraval

Veraval is a noisy, unbearably smelly and unattractive town which provides a base for visiting the Hindu pilgrimage centre of Somnath at Prabhas Patan. Its importance now is as a fishing port – hence the stench. Seagoing *dhows* and fishing boats are still being built by the sea without the use of any modern instruments, traditional skills being passed down from father to son.

Prabhas Patan (Somnath)

Somnath Temple ① *6 km east of Veraval, puja at 0700, 1200 and 1900*, a major Hindu pilgrimage centre, is said to have been built out of gold by Somraj, the Moon God (and subsequently in silver, wood and stone). In keeping with the legend, the stone façade appears golden at sunset. Mahmud of Ghazni plundered it and removed the gates in 1024. Destroyed by successive Muslim invaders, it was rebuilt on the same spot. The final reconstruction did not take place until 1950 and is still going on. Unfortunately, it lacks character but it has been built to traditional patterns with a soaring 50-m-high tower that rises in clusters. Dedicated to Siva, it has one of the 12 sacred *jyotirlingas*. You cannot take bags of any kind, cameras or mobiles into the temple.

Nearby is the ruined **Rudreshvara Temple**, which dates from the same time as the Somnath Temple and was laid out in a similar fashion. The sculptures on the walls and doorways give an indication of what the original Somnath Temple was like. There is a really old Shiva Linga here – very atmospheric temple.

Krishna was believed to have been hit by an arrow, shot by the Bhil, Jara, when he was mistaken for a deer at Bhalka Teerth, and was cremated at Triveni Ghat, east of Somnath.

Diu → *For listings, see pages 117-128. Phone code: 02875. Population: 21,600.*

The island of Diu has a fascinating history and a relaxed atmosphere with little traffic. The north side of the island has salt pans and marshes which attract wading birds, the south coast has some limestone cliffs and pleasant, sandy beaches. Although often compared to Goa, it is nowhere near as picturesque. The island is still visited by relatively few foreign

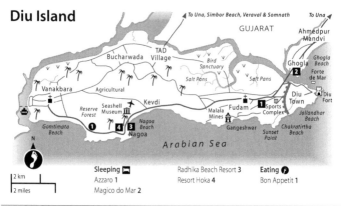

Diu Island

Sleeping	Radhika Beach Resort 3	Eating
Azzaro 1	Resort Hoka 4	Bon Appetit 1
Magico do Mar 2		

travellers though its tavernas attract those deprived of alcohol from neighbouring Gujarat and the bars can get noisy especially at the weekend. It can be quite intimidating for women. It's no paradise island, but if you're in the area it offers a welcome break from the rigours of travelling around Gujarat. Most hotels cater for Gujarati families and so can be noisy. Diu town however has a relaxed vibe, crumbling charm and friendly locals.

Information is available from the **Tourist Complex** ① *Ghogla, Mon-Fri 0930-1315, 1400-1745*, or the **Information Assistant** ① *Diu jetty north of Bunder Chowk, T02875-252653, www.diuindia.com.*

Background

Like Daman across the gulf, Diu was a Portuguese colony until 1961. In 1987 its administration was separated from Goa (some 1600 km away), which then became a State – Diu remains a Union Territory. From the 14th to 16th centuries the sultans of Oman held the reins of maritime power here. The Portuguese failed to take Diu at their first attempt in 1531 but succeeded three years later. Like Daman, it was once a port for the export of opium from Malwa (Madhya Pradesh) but with the decline of Portugal as a naval power it became little more than a backwater.

About 5000 of the elders here (out of a population of 40,000) still speak fluent Portuguese. There are around 200 Catholic families and the local convent school teaches English, Gujarati, Portuguese and French. The Divechi people remain eligible for Portuguese passports and a few apply daily. Many families have a member working in Lisbon or former Portuguese Africa.

Diu town

The small town is squeezed between the fort on the east and a large city wall to the west. With its attractively ornamented buildings and its narrow streets and squares, it has more of a Portuguese flavour than Daman. While some visitors find it quite dirty and decaying, and are disappointed by the number of liquor shops, others find Diu an enjoyable little place. The night market is a great place to have a drink and to wander around.

St Paul's Church (1601-1610), on Travessa dos Hospital, the road running from the fort, has a fine baroque façade, impressive wood panelling and an attractive courtyard. At this church, take the left-hand turning on to Rua de Isabel Fernandes for the **Church of St Francis of Assisi** (1593), part of which is a hospital (a doctor is available at 0930 for a free consultation). On Rua de Torres Novas is **St Thomas's Church** ① *0800-2000*, housing the museum with an interesting local collection. It has been renovated and now houses stone sculptures, woodcarvings and shadow clocks, as well as a café and pleasant rooms to let. These, and the fort, are floodlit at night.

Diu Fort (1535-1541) ① *0700-1800*, considered to be one of Asia's foremost Portuguese forts, was built after the Mughal Emperor Humayun attacked the Sultan of Gujarat with the help of the Portuguese. Until 1960 it garrisoned 350 Portuguese soldiers. Skirted by the sea on three sides and a rock-cut canal on the fourth, it had two moats, one of which was tidal. The lighthouse stands at one end and parts of the central keep are still used as a jail but has few occupants. Despite being damaged, some of the structures – walls, gateways, arches, ramps, bastions – still give us an idea of the formidable nature of the defences. It's worth allowing an hour for a visit.

Makata Lane or **Panchwati**, near the Zampa gate, has some impressive old mansions of rich Portuguese and Indian merchants ranging from Venetian Gothic-style bungalows to traditional carved wooden or stone *havelis*.

Forte de Mar

Forte de Mar (Fortress of Panikot), built in 1535, was strategically important as an easily defended base for controlling the shipping lanes on the northeast part of the Arabian Sea. It has a lighthouse and a chapel to Our Lady of the Sea. It can be approached from Diu jetty when canoes or motor boats are available although landing is not permitted at present. The other fort at the eastern end of the island guarded the mint, while two others once guarded the west at Vanakbara and the bay to the south at Nagoa.

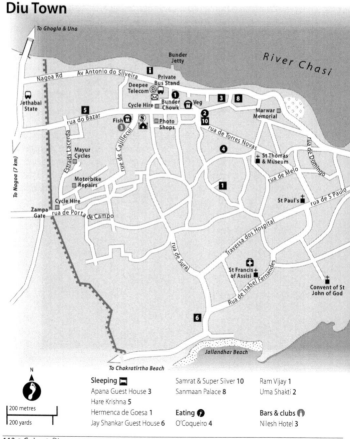

Diu Town

Sleeping
Apana Guest House 3
Hare Krishna 5
Hermenca de Goesa 1
Jay Shankar Guest House 6

Samrat & Super Silver 10
Sanmaan Palace 8

Eating
O'Coqueiro 4

Ram Vijay 1
Uma Shakti 2

Bars & clubs
Nilesh Hotel 3

200 metres
200 yards

Bird sanctuary

The creeks to the north of Diu island have been declared a bird sanctuary. There are watchtowers to spot flocks of shore birds including oyster-catchers, sanderlings and plovers. Lots of herons and ibises, flamingos, pelicans, etc, visit seasonally. Jackals, jungle cats and porcupines are seen in the evening.

Beaches

Several beaches on the south side of Diu Island are easy to get to from Diu town by cycle or auto-rickshaw. Beaches between Nagoa and Vanakbara are safe all year except between May and July and are often empty, as is the beach along Ghogla. However, beware of the giant thorns that are hazardous to cycle tyres.

Jallandhar Beach, to the south, is pleasant and the nearest to Diu. There have been several reports of groups of teenage boys, who not only come to watch and pester tourists but aggressively offer sex.

Chakratirtha Beach, just southwest, has a sunset view point, an open auditorium and a small beach which has been spoiled by the glut of beachside cabins.

Just east of Diu Town **Fudam** (or Fofrara) has the air of a Portuguese village with the crumbling Church of Our Lady of the Remedies. **Malala Mines** are limestone quarries off the Nagoa road. **Gangeshwar Temple** nearby has an attractive *Nandi* and Siva *linga* washed by the sea at high tide.

About 7 km from town, facing the Arabian Sea, **Nagoa** offers the best location for a quiet stay away from Diu town. Its semi-circular palm-fringed beach suitable for swimming is popular with foreigners but also large numbers of Indian tourists who come to watch. There are quieter beaches nearby and the forests are pleasant for walks although the entire stretch from Nagoa is being landscaped for development. A **sea shell museum** ⓘ *Rs 10*, has opened on the road from the airport to Nagoa. It displays a large number of mollusc and crustacean shells, corals and marine life from all over the world, collected by a retired merchant navy captain.

The fishing village of **Ghogla-Ahmedpur Mandvi** on the mainland is also part of Diu. Its name changes to Ahmedpur Mandvi on crossing to the Gujarat side of the border. The beach is good for swimming and it has splendid views of fishing villages and the fort and churches on Diu island. **Jyoti Watersports** and **Magico Do Mar** offer a variety of watersports here including parasailing, speed boating and waterskiing. Beware of the rip tide just a few metres out to sea, which has claimed several lives.

Bucharwada, to the north, lacks attractive beaches but has cheap spartan rooms in Viswas Hotel. **Gomtimata**, a secluded white sand beach to the west, is where a **Tourist Hostel** is expected to open – but no evidence at time of writing. **Vanakbara**, the fishing village on the western tip of the island, has the Church of Our Lady of Mercy. Get to the early-morning fish market and watch the colourful trawlers unload catches of shark, octopus and every kind of fish imaginable. The drying fish on 'washing lines' and waterside activities provide photo opportunities. You can also watch traditional *dhow* building.

There is a ferry service across to Gomtimata. **Simbor Beach** is a pleasant and little-known beach. It is 27 km from Diu town, off the Una road, and can be reached in 45 minutes from Diu by hiring a moped or scooter. Take food and water.

Porbandar → *For listings, see pages 117-128. Phone code: 0286. Population 133,000.*

The former capital of the Jethwa Rajput petty princely state, Porbandar was previously named Sudamapuri, after Krishna's devoted friend, and has a temple dedicated to her. The *dhow*-building tradition that continues on the seashore to the present day reflects a history of maritime trade with North Africa and Arabia. Today, Porbandar is closely associated with Mahatma Gandhi and is also known for its production of gold and silver trinkets, fine-quality silk and cotton manufacture and chemical and cement factories.

Mahatma Gandhi was born in Porbandar in 1869. Next to the family home with its carved balconies is **Kirti Mandir** ① *sunrise-sunset, but the guide takes a lunch break from 1300-1400*, a small museum that traces his life and contains memorabilia and a library. **Darbargadh**, a short walk from Kirti Mandir, the old palace of the Maharanas of Porbandar, was built in the 1780s but is now deserted. It has some intricate carvings and carved balconies; the rooms inside (if you can get in) have interesting paintings. **Sartanji** (or Rana-no) **Choro** (1785), near the ST stand, is the beautiful pleasure pavilion of Maharajah Sartanji, a great poet, writer and music lover. The pavilion has domes, pillars and carved arches and its four sides represent the four seasons. The Maharana's deserted sprawling **Hazur Palace** is near the seafront. Ask for permission to visit the rooms inside at the office. **Daria Rajmahal**, the splendid turn-of-the-century palace of the Maharana of Porbandar, now a college, has intricate carvings, courtyards, fountains, carved arches and heavily embellished façades. The tower has excellent views of the seashore. **Chaya**, 2 km from Chowpatty sea face, is the old capital of the Jetwas. The **Darbargadh Palace** with a beautiful carved balcony, is believed to have secret tunnels and passages to temples and places of safety.

The **Bharat Mandir Hall** in Dayananda Vatika garden is across the Jubilee (Jyubeeli) Bridge. It has a large marble relief map of India on the floor and bas reliefs of heroes from Hindu legends on the pillars. Nearby **Arya Kanya Gurukul** is an experiment in education for girls based on ancient Indian tradition. The dated **planetarium** has shows in Gujarati only. The architecture incorporates different religious styles illustrating Gandhi's open mind.

Jhavar Creek attracts scores of waterbirds. Flamingos, pelicans, storks and heron can be seen from the road in the mangrove marshes. Fisheries have appeared around the creek where the fish put out to dry attract thousands of terns and gulls.

Jamnagar and around → For listings, see pages 117-128. Phone code: 0288. Population: 447,700.

Jamnagar, now an expanding town, was a 16th-century pearl fishing centre with one of the biggest pearl fisheries in the world until the early 20th century. The famous cricketer Ranjitsinghji was its ruler from 1907-1933.

The walled city is famous for its embroidery, silverware and *bandhani* (tie-dye) fabrics produced in workshops in the narrow lanes. **Pirotan Island** in the middle of the Ranmal lake in the Old City, reached by a stone bridge, has the **Lakhota Fort** and **Kotha Bastion** ⓘ *Thu-Tue 1030-1300, 1500-1730, closed 2nd and 4th Sun*, with its arsenal. The **Fort Museum** has a collection of sculpture and pottery found in ruined medieval villages nearby. It is also a pleasant, cool and quiet spot just to relax while listening to the strains of

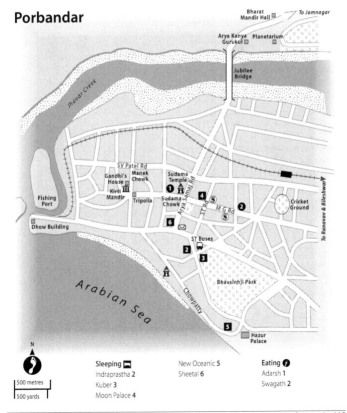

Porbandar

Sleeping 🛌
Indraprastha 2
Kuber 3
Moon Palace 4

New Oceanic 5
Sheetal 6

Eating 🍴
Adarsh 1
Swagath 2

Shri Ram, Jai Ram, Jai Jai Ram wafting across the lake from the **Bala Hanuman Temple**. The temple is worth a visit, especially early evening. The bastion has an old well from which water can be drawn by blowing into a small hole in the floor. The **solarium** uses solar radiation to cure diseases. A group of **Jain temples** in the Old City are profusely decorated with glass, gilding and mirrors.

Northwest of the town centre is the **Ayurvedic University** ① *T0288-266 4866, www.ayurveduniversity.com*, at present the only one in India, which teaches courses to bachelor and postgraduate level in Ayurvedic medicine and yoga. A limited number of places are available for suitably qualified foreign students.

Khijadia Lakes ① *10 km northeast of Jamnagar, US$5; car with up to 6 passengers US$20; camera US$5, professional still camera US$10, video US$500; guide US$5*, are three freshwater lakes surrounded by salt pans and salt marshes. Entirely flooded in the wet season, the lakes remain fresh throughout the dry season, though they occasionally dry out completely. The lakes, a bird sanctuary, are an important staging post for migratory birds, including swallows, martins and wagtails, and many waterfowl.

Marine National Park ① *30 km away, same price as Khijadia Lakes*, offshore from the southern coast of the Gulf of Kachchh, comprises an archipelago of 42 islands noted for their coral reefs and mangroves. It is possible to see dolphins, finless porpoise and sea turtles and a variety of colourful tropical fish. The area also attracts a host of waterbirds. The best island to visit is 1.5-sq-km **Pirotan**. To get there hire motor boats for 15-45 people from Jamnagar jetty (or from Okha) and take a guide. Permits are needed and are available from the Director, Marine National Park, Rajdarshan Ground, Jamnagar. Pirotan is uninhabited except for lighthouse staff.

Dwarka → *For listings, see pages 117-128. Phone code: 02892. Population: 33,600.*

A small coastal town on the tip of the Kathiawad Peninsula, Dwarka is one of the most sacred sites for Vaishnavite Hindus. It has the unique distinction of being one of Hinduism's four 'Holy Abodes' as well as one of its seven 'Holy Places'. Heavily geared up to receive pilgrims, the people are easy going, friendly and welcoming, even to the rarely seen tourist. The beach is good but without any palms for shade.

Archaeological excavations indicate that present-day Dwarka is built on the sites of four former cities. Work in 1990 by the marine archaeologist SR Rao discovered triangular anchors weighing 250 kg similar to those used in Cyprus and Syria during the Bronze Age, suggesting that ships of up to 120 tonnes had used the port around the 14th century BC. Marine research in early 2002 revealed evidence of a substantial city off the coast more than 100 m below current sea level, reviving the debate about the origins of Dwarka's offshore archaeological sites.

The present town mostly dates from the 19th century when Gaekwad princes developed Dwarka as a popular pilgrimage centre. Celebrated as Krishna's capital after his flight from Mathura, thousands come for Krishna's birthday and at Holi and Diwali.

The 12th-century **Rukmini Temple** has beautifully carved *mandapa* columns and a fine sanctuary doorway, but much else is badly weathered. The mainly 16th-century **Dwarkadisha Temple** ① *0600-1200, 1700-2100*, was supposedly built in one night, and some believe that the inner sanctum is 2500 years old. The sanctuary walls probably date from the 12th century. The exterior is more interesting. The soaring five-storey tower is supported by 60 columns. Non-Hindus may enter after completing a form to show some level of commitment to Hinduism and to Krishna, but no photography is allowed inside and cameras must be left at the entrance. Some visitors are approached for a minimum donation of Rs 100. A **lighthouse** ① *1600-1800 or 1 hr before sunset, whichever is earlier, Rs 1, no photography*, stands to the west of the temples. The good-humoured keepers may treat you to a free private guided tour in exchange for any foreign coin (they all 'collect'). The views are beautiful; it's a very peaceful place to rest a while.

Outside Dwarka, the **Nageshwar Mandir** contains one of the 12 *jyotirlingas* in an underground sanctum. It helps to be agile if you wish to catch a glimpse. **Gopi Talav Teerth** is associated with Krishna (and Arjun) and has several shrines in the complex.

Okha
A small port at the head of the Gulf of Kachchh, Okha is 32 km north of Dwarka. You can visit the Marine National Park by hiring a motor boat from the jetty (see Jamnagar, page 115). A pilgrimage to Dwarka is not complete without a visit to the island of **Beyt Dwarka** off the coast from Okha. This is where Krishna is believed to have resided while Dwarka was his capital. The 19th-century temple complex contains several shrines and images of Krishna and his 56 consorts. Archaeological excavations have revealed Harappan artefacts which date from the second millennium BC.

Saurashtra listings

For Sleeping and Eating price codes and other relevant information, see pages 14-17.

⊜ Sleeping

Rajkot *p100, map p101*
Like many towns in Saurashtra, Rajkot suffers from critical water shortages; limit water use as much as possible. Cleanliness standards in virtually all **$$** hotels and below are poor.
$$$ Imperial Palace, Dr Yagnik Rd, T0281-248 0000, www.theimperialpalace.biz. Smartest business hotel in town, with elaborate lobby, in-room internet ports, indoor and outdoor pools, gym, swish restaurant and well-stocked wine shop (alcohol permit required).
$$ Silver Palace, Gondal Rd, T0281-248 0008, www.hotelsilverpalace.com. Smart and modern rooms, deluxe with bathtub, quieter 'executive' rooms face away from street, good **Flavours** restaurant.
$$-$ Galaxy, Jawahar Rd, T0281-222 2905, www.thegalaxyhotelrajkot.com. Great-value modern hotel with 37 very well-furnished,

clean rooms, most a/c, pleasant roof garden, exchange (including TCs, credit cards), well run, courteous and efficient, no restaurant but room service to bring in food, access by lift only. Does not look promising from the street, but a pleasant surprise once you get upstairs. Courtesy pick-up and drop off from airport.
$ Babha Guest House, Panchnath Rd, T0281-222 0861, hotelbabha@rajkot.com. Small, cleanish rooms, some a/c, excellent vegetarian *thalis*.
$ Hotel Yash, Dhebar Rd, near bus stand, T0281-222 3574. Cheap as chapatti options in this area, not much going for them. Hotel **Yash** is cleanish.
$ Railway Retiring Rooms, 1st floor. 3 rooms (1 a/c), 4-bed dorm, reasonable vegetarian restaurant, good value.
$ Samrat International, 37 Karanpura, T0281-222 2269. Promising lobby belies adequate but unloved rooms, some a/c, vegetarian restaurant, genial staff, exchange, the best-kept option near bus stand.

Gondal p100

Heritage hotels are worth the experience.

$$$ Orchard Palace, Palace Rd, near ST Bus Stand, T02825-220002, www.gondalpalaces.com. Overlooking mango and lime groves, 6 a/c rooms in one wing of palace, with old-fashioned baths, attractive gardens, 35 vintage cars, pool (but little water to fill it), excellent dance shows, mosquito nuisance so burn rings, good food ("bland European dishes; order Indian in advance"). Price includes meals; cheaper without meals. Atmospheric. You can also book through **Northwest Safaries**, www.northwestsafaries.com.

$$$ Riverside Palace, by river Gondali, T02825-220002, www.gondalpalaces.com. 19th-century, with a glassed-in terrace, 11 large, attractive non a/c rooms, 4-poster beds. Similar vibe to **Orchard**, but a little more lacklustre.

$$$ Royal Saloon, in garden near **Orchard Palace**, T02825-220002. Beautifully renovated suite in Maharaja's old train, with drawing and dining rooms and sit-outs on the platform, meals from the **Orchard Palace**. Sheer nostalgia. Highly recommended.

$$-$ Bhuvaneswari Rest House, at Shri Bhuvaneswari Pith Temple, T02825-220968. Atmospheric part of town with 2 resthouse options. The newer build is good and clean but a bit pricey at Rs 1800 a night. In the older building, it's looking pretty run down and in need of an overhaul. *Thali* meals available and the temple and Ayurvedic factory close by is fascinating.

Wankaner p102

$$$-$$ Royal Oasis, T02828-220000, www.heritagehotelsofindia.com. Stepping back in time, this guesthouse of the Ranjitvilas is set in large fruit orchards with original 1930s art deco features. There is a stunning *vaav* (step well) onsite with three intricately carved levels, as well as a beautiful art deco pool, although probably empty most of the time. The rooms are a little past their prime and you can eat dinner in the gardens, although mosquitoes can be a problem.

Bhavnagar p102, map p103

$$$-$$ Nilambag Palace, Ahmedabad Rd, T0278-242 9323, www.nilambagpalace.com. A little faded 1850s palace stuffed with the usual array of hunting trophies, 27 upmarket a/c rooms, long bathrooms with tubs (main palace better than cottage annexe, and twice the price), lobby with intricate woodcarving, chandeliers, royal portraits, grand banquet hall now restaurant, vast gardens with peacocks, beautiful stepped pool.

$$ Narayani Heritage, in grounds of **Nilambag Palace**, T0278-251 3535, narayaniheritage@gmail.com. Plain but spacious rooms in converted boys' school, rooms open on to paved courtyard. Shares facilities of Nilambag Palace, eg pool, tennis court. Odd atmosphere definitely feels like an old school.

$$ Sun 'n' Shine, ST Rd, Panwadi, T0278-251 6131. Decaying exterior but incredibly grandiose lobby. Average a/c rooms; those with marble floors are better, reasonably clean throughout, smart and popular vegetarian restaurant, gym, sauna, travel desk, internet.

$ Vrindavan, Darbargadh, T0278-251 9149. Sprawling buildings, part of the old Darbargadh complex (18th-19th century) converted to a budget hotel, 100 rooms, some with baths, a few have Western toilets, some a/c, also Rs 50 dorm beds, a/c Gujarati restaurant (*thali* Rs 50), rather noisy surroundings.

Velavadar National Park p103

$ Kaliyar Bhuvan Forest Lodge, reserve at Forest Office in Bhavnagar, T0278-242 6425. Simple but adequate, 5 small rooms, reasonably furnished, but prohibitively priced for foreigners. Food is also over-priced for foreigners.

Palitana *p104*

Difficult to find cheap rooms but dorm beds are Rs 20-50.

$$$ Vijay Vilas Palace (Heritage Hotel), in Adpur, a cattle herders' village ringed by hills, book ahead through **North West Safaries**, T079-263 08031, www.northwestsafaries.com. 6 rooms in lovely 1906 lodge with Italian country-house feel, surrounded by greenery. Delicious home-cooked Indian meals (non-residents Rs 250 with advance notice). The shorter but steeper route to the Palitana temple complex starts about 200 m away at the temple in Adpur village (follow the milkmaids carrying curd!). 7 km from town (rickshaws Rs 75, shared motorbike-rickshaws Rs 6), tricky to find after dark.

$ Shravak, opposite Central Bus Station, T02848-252428. 18 rooms with baths (Western toilets, hot shower), cheaper with Indian toilet. Better than expected.

$ Sumeru (Gujarat Tourism), Station Rd, near bus stand, T02848-252327. Typical **Gujarat Tourism** vibe – lacklustre, 16 rooms, 4 a/c, 16 dorm beds (Rs 75) with cold water only, limited menu restaurant, tourist office, checkout 0900.

$ Patel House, Station Rd, T02848-242441. Run by private farmer's trust, rather basic and impersonal but set around an open courtyard that shuts off some of the traffic noise, double rooms (cold taps, hot water in buckets, Indian toilet), some 4- and 6-bedded.

Junagadh *p106, map p107*

Rates double during Diwali (Oct-Nov) when large number of Indians visit Girnar.

$$-$ The Lotus Hotel, Station Rd, T0285-265 8500, www.thelotushotel.com. Almost chic, this very white hotel has a nice vibe, Wi-Fi and 24-hr room service.

$$-$ Vishala, 3rd floor, Dhara Complex, opposite ST Bus Stand, T0285-263 1599. Bright and modern rooms, some veering towards contemporary, some with quite eccentric bamboo decor in good new hotel,

uncrowded dorm, quite clean, friendly staff, internet, high enough above street to avoid worst of traffic noise. Good rooftop restaurant. Recommended.

$ Girnar, Majwadi Darwaja, 2 km north, T0285-262 1201. Run by **Gujarat Tourism**. 24 decent rooms, some a/c with bath, best with balcony, dorm (Rs 75), unattractive building but in good location, poor management.

$ Madhuwati, Kalwa Chowk, T0285-262 0087. Noisy location above a shopping complex, 27 spacious rooms, some a/c, attached bath (hot showers in winter only), clean, comfortable, courteous staff. Rooms are OK but the entrance feels unsafe.

$ Railway Retiring Rooms. Clean and well maintained.

$ Relief, Dhal Rd, T0285-262 0280. 14 rooms (some share bath), hot water, 2 a/c, snacks available, untrained but friendly staff, polite owner can help with excursions.

Sasan Gir National Park *p108*

$$$ Vassavo, Sangodra Village, T02877-285 971, www.vibranthotels.net. Innovative design, cottages dotted around central lawn. Cottages are airy with gardens behind glass as your headboard. Bathrooms have private outdoor shower. Lovely decor throughout. Some with river view. Price includes breakfast, lunch, dinner and 1 safari.

$$$-$$ Lion Safari Camp, near Hirenshwar Temple, Chitrod, T02877-296 507, www.campsofindia.com. Characterful tents with a/c and stylish bathrooms. Nice atmosphere.

$$$-$$ Maneland Jungle Lodge, 2 km north of Sasan, T02877-285555, www.maneland.com. Well-appointed suites in bungalow (VIP faces jungle), and rooms in cottages resembling royal hunting lodges, restaurant with limited menu, delightfully designed but needs a bit of a facelift, jungle ambience, lions and panthers heard and occasionally spotted nearby, rich birdlife, wildlife videos.

$$$ Gir Birding Lodge, 1.5 km north of Sasan down dirt track, T02877-295514, www.gir birdinglodge.com, or reserve with **North West Safaries**, see page 78. Clean and comfortable cottages and a 2-bedroom suite downstairs in the main lodge, set in a mango orchard over the wall from the national park. Good naturalist guides available, good buffet breakfast served on veranda looking over wall into forest, lots of langurs, leopards occasionally seen. Beautiful views as you sit on your balcony in the orchard. Highly recommended.

$$ Sinh Sadan Forest Lodge (Govt), T02877-285540. Ridiculously overpriced and run-down rooms (foreigners US$50), with Indian toilets, better a/c chalets (US$75), tents with shared bath, 30-bed dorm (US$5). Food is equally over-priced for foreigners. You can find much better value.

$$-$ Gir Jungle Lodge (Govt), T02877-285 600, www.girjungle.com. New build with basic rooms, still a bit rough around edges needs some finishing touches and maybe the prices will increase when they are done. Bonus is a good ayurvedic centre with full range of treatments at good prices on-site.

$ Nitin Ratangayra Family Rooms, near Sasan bus stop and Umang, T02877-285686. Just 5 basic rooms but cleaner than most and friendly.

$ Umang, near Sasan bus stop, T02877-285728. Has a backdrop of the sanctuary but a crowded village on one side (calls from the mosque disturb the peace). 9 basic rooms in varying states of decay with mediocre baths, rooftop dining room (order meal well ahead), jeep safaris, knowledgeable owner can help with visits to the sanctuary.

Somnath and Veraval *p110*
Mostly you would stay in Veraval to visit temple at Somnath but now there are some new build hotels on the Somnath by-pass road.

$$-$ Hotel Ambar, Somnath by-pass, T02876-231 358, www.hotelambar.in.

Charmless modern block with comfortable standard and 'elegance' rooms.

$ Shubh Suvidha, Kamal Park, Somnath by-pass, T02876-231695. Modern block with comfortable a/c and non a/c rooms available. Best value of the slew of identikit hotels in the area.

$ Madhuram, Junagadh Rd, Veraval, T02876-221938. Comfortable rooms, some a/c, taxis, travel desk, small cafeteria (limited menu), dorms, run down.

Prabhas Patan *p110*
$ Mayuram, Triveni Rd, T02876-231286. Acceptable rooms, good restaurant, clean.

$ Shri Somnath Guest House, near temple, T02876-220212. Has 20 very basic rooms.

Diu *p110, maps p110 and p112*
Most places are basic. Some have a/c rooms with TV and charge double for these, but offer good discounts in low season. High season: Diwali, Christmas/New Year and Apr-May.

$$$ Azzaro, Fofrara, Diu–Nagoa Rd, Fudam, T02875-255 421, www.azzarodiu.com. Stylish lobby and smart looking rooms with chic fabrics and flatscreen TVs – all a/c. Pool is nice, although doesn't quite fit with the decor of the rest of the place.

$$$-$$ Magico do Mar, Ghogla-Ahmedpur Mandvi, T02875-252116, www.magico domar.com. Lovely a/c huts with traditional vibe, Saurashtrian decor and mirrorwork, around a 1930s mansion of a Junagadh Nawab (best Nos 510-513), cheaper non-a/c rooms in unimpressive bungalow, fantastic views, good access to beach, some water sports. Recommended.

$$$-$$ Radhika Beach Resort, Nagoa, close to the beach, T02875-252555, www.radhikaresort.com. 24 comfortable a/c rooms in modern villas, a/c restaurant, good pool in well-tended garden, prompt service, small provisions store handy for beach.

$$ The Resort Hoka, 100 m from the beach among Hoka palms and trees at Nagoa,

T02875-253036, www.resorthoka.com.
10 decent rooms with bath, 3 with shared facilities, clean, pleasant garden, restaurant serves excellent fresh fish, bar, laundry, travel, environment-conscious and friendly management, discounts for long stays, not luxurious but pleasant and good value.

$$ Sanmaan Palace, Pensao Beira Mar Building, Fort Rd, T02875-253031. Pleasant colonial house, sea-facing balcony, 6 rooms and suites, rooftop restaurant. With so many modern places, nice to see some old world charm.

$$ Sugati Beach, Ghogla-Ahmedpur Mandvi, T02875-252212, www.sugatibeachresort.com. Cluster of attractive good-sized bungalows, well-appointed, clean a/c rooms, restaurant, bar, terrace opens onto beach and sea, lacks atmosphere.

$$-$ Apana Guest House, Old Fort Rd, T02875-253650. Has 29 clean rooms, 4 a/c, some with bath (best with TV, hot water, sea view and balcony) and dorm, can be noisy (mainly from Hindi films) especially at weekends, roadside terrace with restaurant and bar.

$$-$ Samrat, Collectorate Rd, T02875-252354. 12 clean rooms, 3 a/c, balconies, good restaurant, helpful manager.

$ Church Hostel, in the old Fudam church. Simple rooms (Rs 100), use of kitchen, very quiet and pleasant.

$ Heranca Goesa, behind Diu Museum, T02875-253851. Very popular relaxed place with local family. Serving leisurely breakfasts and slap-up fish suppers with Goan and Portuguese influences – step in even if you don't score a room here.

$ Jay Shankar Guest House, 1 min from Jallandhar Beach, T02875-252424. Small dorm (Rs 50), backpacker abode with some cleanish rooms – look around to pick the best of the bunch. There's alcohol on sale downstairs which might help with some of the dingier rooms.

$ Super Silver, near Samrat and Foreign Market, T02875-252020, hotel_supersilver diu@yahoo.com. Clean basic rooms, no frills but good value, some with a/c. Internet café and shops in complex downstairs.

Porbandar *p114, map p115*

$$-$ Kuber, Bhavsinhji Park, near ST station, T0286-224 1024. Most of the 19 rooms have a/c, suites with fridge, friendly and helpful manager, free airport transfer. Recommended.

$$-$ Sheetal, Arya Samaj Rd, opposite GPO, T0286-224 8341. Some a/c rooms with shower or tub, 24-hr "homely" food service. They pride themselves on home comforts.

$ Indraprastha, near ST Station, T0286-224 2681. Large modern hotel, comfortable, all the usual features, some a/c.

$ Moon Palace, ST Rd, near Bhavsinhji Park, ST Rd, T0286-224 1172, moonpalace@ mail.com. Clean, cosy rooms with bath.

$ New Oceanic, 8 Chowpatty, T0286-224 2917. Sea views, modern, 17 rooms, some a/c, good garden restaurant (Western, Indian) but rather expensive. Downstairs rooms bit dingier, so aim for second floor.

Jamnagar *p115*

$$$ Express Hotel, Motikhavdi, Sikka, 21 km down Dwarka Rd, T0288-234 4416, www.expressworld.com. 117 centrally a/c rooms in modern hotel with good business facilities .

$$$-$$ Aram (Heritage Hotel), Pandit Nehru Rd, 3 km northwest of centre, T0288-255 1701. Good a/c rooms in 1940s character mansion (bit garish), Raj memorabilia, pleasant vegetarian garden restaurant, friendly, good service. At time of writing, under renovation so maybe prices will go up.

$ Aashiana, New Supermarket, Bedi Gate, 3rd floor, T0288-255 9110, www.ashiana hotel.com. 34 rooms, 14 clean a/c rooms with TV, better than the competition, simple restaurant serving inexpensive Indian vegetarian, good value.

$ President, Teen Batti, T0288-255 7491, www.hotelpresident.in. 48 bright, spacious rooms, most a/c, some with balcony, relaxing a/c restaurant (efficient service), internet.
$ Relax, opposite Town Hall, T0288-255 6115. Good clean rooms – great value. And for boys, very nice dorms (they are mixed dorms but cannot imagine ladies wanting to stay in a dorm). Dorms just Rs 250.

Dwarka *p116*
$$-$ Dwarka Residency, near ISKCON gate, T02892-235032, www.dwarkaresidency.com. Smart, modern business hotel hiding behind quirky 'robotic' façade, with comfortable a/c rooms and a salubrious restaurant. Website is quite cosmic too.
$ Meera, near railway station, T02892-234031. Friendly, excellent *thalis*.
$ Satnam Wadi, near the beach. Rooms with bath and sea view.
$ Toran (Gujarat Tourism), near Govt Guest House, T02892-234013. 12 clean, well-maintained rooms with nets, dorm (Rs 75), courteous service, checkout 0900, "dedicated and friendly manager". Recommended.

🍴 Eating

Rajkot *p100, map p101*
$$ Havmor, Jawahar Rd, near **Galaxy Hotel** (see Sleeping). Good non-vegetarian food (varied menu, mainly Chinese), a/c but a bit fly-ridden.
$$ Lakshmi Lodge in road opposite **Rainbow**, see below. Good *thalis*.
$ Rainbow Lakhajiraj Rd. Good South Indian, also very busy in the evenings.
$ Shakti Vijay, various locations including Dheba Rd and Sadar Rd. Delicious home-made ice creams, recommended.
$ Thaker Lodge, Kanta Sree Vikas Gruh Rd, T0281-222 1836. Highly regarded place for local food, often queues to get in at night.

Gondal *p100*
$ Bhajiya shop, near railway station. Sells a variety of delicious vegetarian *pakoras* (*bhajiya*) with dips, pickles and chutneys.
$ Dreamland, Kailash Complex, ST Rd. First-class unlimited Gujarati and Punjabi *thalis*, served in separate rooms, delightfully cool a/c.

Bhavnagar *p102, map p103*
Sweet shops around Piramal Chowk and Waghawadi Rd sell melt-in-the mouth *pedas* and *sangam*, a cashew nut candy, as well as savoury snacks like Bhavnagar *ganthias*.
$ Greenland, Krishnanagar, near Barton Museum. North Indian and ice creams in a pleasant garden setting.
$ Murli, Panwadi Chowk. Excellent *thalis*.
$ Nilambag Palace (see Sleeping). Banquet Hall (chandeliers, Belgian mirrors, Burma teak furniture). Wide choice of mainly non-vegetarian tandoori food. Garden restaurant at night is pleasant, except for loud Hindi film music.
$ Tulsi, Kalanala Chowk. An attractive little restaurant, with subtle lighting and good, mainly North Indian food.

Palitana *p104*
Many eateries in Taleti Rd offer Gujarati *thali* as well as *pau-bhaji* and ice cream. Along Station Rd, *thalis* are Rs 10-15.
$ Mansi Park, Bhavnagar Rd. North Indian, Chinese. Pleasant open-air restaurant, tables on the lawn and in kiosks, hill views (main dishes Rs 35-50), also tea-time treats (cheese toast, finger chips, *iddli*, *dosa*).

Junagadh *p106, map p107*
Near **Kalwa Chowk**, try *dal-pakwana* (a Sindhi brunch), stuffed parathas, fruit juices (*kesar* mango Apr-Jun). In **Azad Chowk**, try milk sweets, snacks and curds.

$$ Garden Café, Girnar Rd. Attractive outdoor restaurant with view of hills, flowering plants and lawns, average food, good atmosphere and service; handy for visitors to the hill.

$ Geeta and **Sharda**, both near railway station. Good *thalis*.

$ Poonam, Dhal Rd, Chittakhana Chowk, 1st floor. Unlimited Gujarati *thalis* (Rs 35-60). Excellent food and service.

$ Sagar, Jayshree Talkies Rd. Good Punjabi and Gujarati, vegetarian, Indian breakfast (*puri-sabzi*), *idly*, *lassi*.

$ Santoor, off MG Rd, near Kalwa Chowk, upstairs. 0945-1500, 1700-2300. Very good Indian and Chinese vegetarian dishes, a/c, excellent value.

$ Swati, Jayshree Talkies Rd. Mainly Punjabi, some South Indian and Chinese, all vegetarian. Good food and *lassi*, courteous, enthusiastic staff, clean and comfortable, a/c, one of the town's most popular restaurants.

Veraval *p110*

$ Ali Baba, near Park Hotel (see Sleeping). Recommended for seafood.

$ Sagar, Riddhi-Siddhi Complex, 1st floor, between bus stand and clock tower. A/c, excellent service, vegetarian Punjabi and South Indian.

Diu *p110, maps p110 and p112*

Some Catholic homes serve traditional Portuguese food to Western travellers with an hour's notice (ask directions in the Christian locality near St Paul's Church).

$$ Apana, Old Fort Rd. Large seafood platters (shark, lobster, kingfish, crab and vegetarian), Rs 300, easily shared by 4-6. Recommended.

$$ Bon Appetite, Nagoa–Gomti road, 1 km from Nagoa Beach, T09879593713. Chilled out place with floor seating, offering up a range of fresh fish and a small selection of other fare. Phone to order pizzas from the wood-oven or a barbecue.

$$-$ O'Coqueiro, Firangiwada Rd, near Diu Museum, T(0)9824-681565. Serving up a range of great fish curries or try grilled fish and coriander potatoes. There's a great selection of veg and chicken dishes too, but seafood is where it's at. Chilled out vibe and super friendly family. Recommended.

$$-$ Radhika Beach Resort, Nagoa. Wide choice of Indian, Chinese, some continental. Well-prepared meals from spotless kitchen, a/c and attentive service. Not much of a vibe though.

$ Martha's Place, opposite the museum. Excellent home-cooking, good views.

$ Ram Vijay, Bundi Chowk, near State Bank of Saurashtra. Excellent 'home-made' ice creams – coconut and date 'n' almond are particularly good, milk shakes and sodas, friendly.

$ Uma Shakti, near Samrat. Good food and service (try toasted cheese sandwiches).

Porbandar *p114, map p115*

Sudama Chowk near the ST Stand is where locals gather for samosas, *pakodas, bhel, kachori, pau bhaji*, etc, in the evening.

$ Adarsh, MG Rd. A/c, Indian vegetarian and ice creams.

$ Khana Khazana, MG Rd. Open sunset to past midnight. Recommended for cheese and chutney sandwiches, cheese toasts, burgers and coffee; South Indian snacks (hot *idlis*) on Sun. Also takeaway.

$ Swagath, MG Rd. Excellent *thalis*, pleasant. The bazar sells *khajli* (fried dough snack), *thabdi* and *peda* (milk sweets).

Jamnagar *p115*

$$ Rangoli, near Anupam Talkies, near Bedi Gate. Open lunchtime and evening (except Wed). A/c, good but pricier vegetarian Punjabi and South Indian, friendly.

$ Kalpana, near Teen Batti. Vegetarian dishes.

$ Urvee, Supermarket, Town Hall Rd. Good Gujarati *thalis* at lunch time.

Dwarka p116

Poor choice of rather dirty eating places, best to eat in one of the hotels.
Dwarkeshwar is best for tasty, hygienic *thalis* but slow service.

🎵 Bars and clubs

Diu p110, maps p110 and p112

The night market, near the post office, is very popular. Kingfisher, Turbo, London Pilsner, Rs 20-30 per bottle; tasty snacks from stalls too. Most bars close around 2130.
Nilesh, stays open until 2300.

⚙ Festivals and events

Palitana p104

Mar Teras Fair at Gheti (Adpur-Palitana, 4 km from town) 3 days before **Holi**. Thousands of Jain pilgrims attend, joined by villagers who come for free lunches.

Junagadh p106, map p107

Feb-Mar Bhavnath Fair at Sivaratri at Damodar Kund near the Girnar foothills is very spectacular. Attended by *naga bawas* (naked sages), who often arrive on decorated elephants to demonstrate strange powers (including the strength of their penis), and colourful tribal people who come to worship and perform *Bhavai* folk theatre.
Nov-Dec A popular 10-day **fair** is held at the Jain temples starting at Kartik Purnima.

Dwarka p116

Aug/Sep Janmashtami. Special worship and **fair** (Aug).

🛍 Shopping

Bhavnagar p102, map p103

Textiles, locally embroidered cushion covers, shawls, *bandhni* and mock-silver jewellery are good buys. Try **Vora Bazar**, **Radhanpuri Market**, **Amba Chowk**, **Darbargadh Lane** and **Talao** fruit and veg market. Handlooms and handicrafts are best at **Khadi stores** in the Barton Museum building.

Palitana p104

Local handicrafts include embroidery (saris, dresses, purses, bags, wall hangings, etc) and metal engraving. You can watch the craftsmen making harmonium reeds.

Diu p110, maps p110 and p112

The night market is very lively in the evenings. Govt **Cottage Emporia** near the jetty sell local crafts of stone, metal and shell; **Jaysukh**, Sangaria Lane, has good shell crafts. Don't be tempted by star tortoise and turtle shell bangles and souvenirs; they are illegal under the Wildlife Protection Act, severe penalties attached. There is a fine second-hand bookshop in **Super Silver Hotel**.

🏔 Activities and tours

Diu p110, maps p110 and p112
Cruises
Evening cruises from Bunder Chowk jetty to Nagoa Beach, with music, Rs 100 per person; enquire at the tourist office.

Tour operators
Oceanic, Bunder Chowk, T02875-252 1800.
Reshma, facing **Nilesh Hotel**, T02875-252241.

Watersports
At Nagoa and Ahmedpur-Mandvi have parasailing, windsurfing, 8-seater speed boats and jet skiing. A pool/water slide complex is next to Kohinoor on the Diu–Nagoa road.

Dwarka p116

Dwarka Darshan. A tour of 4 local pilgrimage sites (Nageshwar Mandir, Gopi Talav Teerth, Beyt Dwarka, Rukmini Temple) by minibus, departs 0800, 1400, 5 hrs (can take 7 people). Tickets Rs 30; book a day in advance for morning tour. Or visit only Beyt Dwarka for a worthwhile day spent with pilgrims.

Rajkot p100, map p101

Air Some 4 km northwest, airline buses run transfers to town. **Indian Airlines**, Angel's Hotel, Dhebar Chowk, T0281-222 2295, airport T0281-245 3313, www.indian-airlines.nic.in. **Jet Airways**, 7 Bilkha Plaza, Kasturba Rd, T0281-247 9623, airport T0281-245 4533, www.jetairways.com, flies to **Mumbai** daily.

Bus The ST bus station is just south of the busy Dhebar Chowk at the centre, with buses to **Junagadh** (2 hrs), **Veraval** (5 hrs), **Jamnagar** (2 hrs), **Dwarka** and **Ahna**. More comfortable private long-distance coaches leave from locations around the city, especially around Shastri Maidan. **Eagle Travels**, 107-108 Yagnik Rd, T0281-304 8611, www.eaglecorporate.com, runs several luxury buses daily to **Ahmedabad**, as well as to **Mount Abu**, **Mumbai**, **Porbandar**, Udaipur and Vadodara. **Jay Somnath Travels**, Umesh Complex, near Chaudhari High School, T0281-243 3315, have 3-4 buses a day to **Bhuj**.

Train Junction Station **Ahmedabad**: *Rajkot Ahmedabad Exp 19154*, 0630, 4¼ hrs; *Saurashtra Exp 19216*, 0045, 6½ hrs (continues to **Vadodara**, 2¾ hrs); *Sau Janta Exp 19018*, 1520, 5¼ hrs (continues to **Vadodara**, 2½ hrs). **Mumbai** (**Central**): *Okha Mumbai Saurashtra Mail 19006*, 1735, 14½ hrs; *Saurashtra Exp 19216*, 0050, 18½ hrs. **Porbandar**: *Saurashtra Exp 19215*, 0135, 4¾ hrs; *Porbandar Exp 19264*, 0825, Mon, Thu, 5 hrs. **Vadodara**: same as Mumbai, 7¼-9 hrs. **Veraval**: *Jabalpur-Veraval Exp 11464*, 1310, 4 hrs.

Bhavnagar p102, map p103

Air The airport is 5 km southeast of town; auto-rickshaws to town insist on Rs 65-75. **Indian Airlines**, T0278-249 3445, airport T0278-249 3130, www.indian-airlines.nic.in, **Jet Airways**, Surat House, Waghawadi Rd,

T0278-243 3371, airport T0278-220 2004, www.jetairways.com, flies to **Mumbai**.

Bus Frequent rickety buses from the ST stand in the New Town. Routes include: **Palitana** (1¾ hrs); several to **Una** for **Diu** (6 hrs); **Velavadar** (1 hr). Private operators: Tanna Travels, Waghawadi Rd, T0278-242 0477, has luxury coaches (reclining seats) to/from **Ahmedabad**, almost hourly from 0600, 4½ hrs plus short tea break, recommended; to **Vadodara**, 5½ hrs, 3 daily. Punjab Travels, Kalanala, T0278-242 4582.

Train The station is in the Old City, about 3 km north of the ST Bus Stand. **Ahmedabad**: a slow journey as the line takes a circuitous route to skirt the marshes; buses are generally preferable. *Bandra Exp 12972*, 12045, 5½ hrs; continues to **Mumbai** (Bandra). Also several local trains.

Velavadar National Park p103

A few buses from Bhavnagar; better to hire a car. Alternatively hire a Jeep/*chhakra* (motorbike trailer) from Vallabhipur on the Ahmedabad–Bhavnagar highway. A new bridge being built near Bhavnagar port to Adhelai near the park will make access faster and easier.

Palitana p104

Bus ST Bus (0800-1200, 1400-1800) to **Ahmedabad** (often with a change at Dhandhuka), deluxe from Ahmedabad (0700, 0800, 0900); to **Bhavnagar** (1½ hrs), **Jamnagar**, **Rajkot**, **Surat**, **Una**, **Vadodara** and **Veraval** (for **Sasan Gir**). Private de luxe coaches to **Surat** and **Mumbai** via **Vadodara**. Operators: **Paras**, Owen Bridge, T02848-252370. Opposite ST depot: **Khodiar**, T02848-252586 (to Surat) and **Shah**, T02848-252396.

Taxi For up to 7 people, run between **Bhavnagar** (57 km by State Highway) and Palitana, Rs 35 per seat.

Train To **Bhavnagar** a few times a day.

Alang *p105*

Buses from ST Bus Stand in Bhavnagar, through the day from 0600 (last return 1800), 1¾ hrs, Rs 25. Taxis take 1½ hrs, Rs 500-600 return, and auto-rickshaws Rs 300-400 with bargaining. At Alang, *tongas* go up and down the beachfront past the shipyards for Rs 7.

Junagadh *p106, map p107*

Bicycle Hire from shops on Dhal Rd, near **Relief Hotel**; Rs 25-30 per day.

Bus Regular buses to **Ahmedabad, Rajkot** (2 hrs), **Veraval, Porbandar** and **Sasan Gir** (2½ hrs). One direct bus to **Palitana**, 0500, 6 hrs; otherwise change at **Songadh** (4 hrs)

Train Ahmedabad: *Somnath Exp 19222*, 2105, 7¼ hrs; *Jabalpur Exp 11463/11465*, 1130, 9 hrs; *Veraval Ahmedabad Exp 19129*, 0843, 7½ hrs; all via **Rajkot**, 2½-3¼ hrs. **Veraval**: *Veraval Exp 11464/11466*, 1536, 1¾ hrs. For **Sasan Gir**: take *Fast Pass 352* to **Delwada**, 0605.

Sasan Gir National Park *p108*

Air Nearest convenient airport is Rajkot.

Bus Service to/from **Junagadh** (54 km), 2½ hrs, and **Veraval** (40 km), 2 hrs. Service to **Una** for **Diu** is unpredictable, morning departure 1100. Occasional buses to **Ahmedabad**.

Train From **Junagadh** to Sasan Gir, *352*, 0650, 3 hrs, continues to **Delwada** near Diu; return to Junagadh, *351*, 1827, so possible to visit for the day. The route is very attractive. **Talala** is the last major station, 15 km before Sasan, so stock up with fruit, biscuits, liquids there. From **Veraval**, take *359* at 1039, or *353* at 1409, both bound for Khijadiya; return to **Veraval**, by *354* at 1138 or *360* at 1535.

Veraval *p110*

Somnath Travels, Satta Bazar, will obtain tickets for long-distance journeys.

Bicycle Hire from opposite bus station or railway station, some in poor condition (road between Veraval and Somnath is appalling).

Bus Buses to **Diu, Porbandar** (2 hrs), **Bhavnagar** (9 hrs). Deepak Ramchand Taxis, T02876-222591 has non-a/c Ambassador taxis. To **Ahmedpur Mandvi** (via docks) and **Somnath** Rs 550, **Diu** Rs 600, tour of docks and Somnath Rs 250.

Taxi Taxis from **Tower Rd** and **ST** bus stands are cheaper than those at the railway station.

Train Train to **Ahmedabad**: *Somnath Exp 19222*, 1900, 11¼ hrs; *Veraval Ahmedabad Exp 19120*, 0630, 10¾ hrs.

Prabhas Patan *p110*

From **Veraval**, auto-rickshaw (bargain to Rs 30 return) or frequent bus.

Diu *p110, maps p110 and p112*

Most visitors arrive by long-distance buses either via Una or direct to the island, easiest from Ahmedabad via Bhavnagar. A road bridge connects Diu Town with Ghogla which has more frequent buses.

Air The airport is 6 km west of the town; auto-rickshaws charge around Rs 50 to transfer. **Jet Airways**, at the airport, Nagoa Rd, T02875-253542, www.jetairways.com, accepts credit card payment. **Mumbai**, daily except Sat.

Bicycle Hire about Rs 50 per day. **A to Z**, near Veg Market, Panchwati Rd; **Shilpa**, Bunder Chowk; **Mayur**, past Ankur Hotel (across rough ground, then 20 m along alley to left), excellent bikes; **Daud**, Zampa Gate, well-maintained, new bikes; **Krishna Cycles** at Ghogla.

Bus Local: Bus stand: to **Nagoa** 3 daily; frequent service to **Bucharwada-Vanakbara** and **Una**, Rs 4 (minibus Rs 6).
Long distance: Most long-distance buses operate from the Jethabai Bus Stand just south of the bridge to Ghogla. ST services to **Ahmedabad** via Bhavnagar, 0700 (10 hrs); **Bhavnagar**, ask for 1035 'direct bus' as some go through Mahuva and are packed; **Jamnagar** via Junagadh, 0600; **Porbandar**, 1300; **Rajkot**, several 0445-1725 (7 hrs); **Vadodara**, 1730; **Veraval**, several 0400-1300 (2½ hrs). Buses often leave 15-20 mins early.

A wider choice of buses serve **Una**, 8 km from Diu on the mainland, connected by local buses and auto-rickshaws.

Private agents in the Main Sq offer buses from the private bus stand to **Mumbai** (1000), **Ahmedabad** (1900) and major towns in Gujarat; often more reliable than ST buses. Goa Travels serve **Bhavnagar**, **Junagadh** (5 hrs) and **Palitana**.

Shiv Shakti, Sahajan and Gayatri Travels run from the main bus station to **Ahmedabad**, **Bhavnagar**, **Mumbai**, **Vadodara**, etc.

Vanakbara, at the west end of the island, has buses to **Okha** via **Veraval**, **Porbandar** and **Dwarka** at 0700 and 0800.

Motorbike Hire in the market area; mopeds, scooters and motorbikes cost from about Rs 140-300 a day plus fuel and deposit. Kismet, T02875-252971, has good new scooters, friendly service. Repairs off Estrada Lacerda.

Rickshaw Auto-rickshaw: Rs 30 to **Nagoa**, Rs 25 to **Ghogla**. Demand Rs 100 to **Una** or **Delwada**.

Train Delvada, 8 km north between Diu and Una, is the nearest railhead just south of Una; auto-rickshaws demand Rs 100 from Diu to Una or Delwada. The station is a short walk from the centre of town – follow the locals. Slow, crowded trains with hard wooden benches go to **Junagadh** via **Sasan Gir**.

Porbandar p114, map p115
Air Jet Airways, T0286-222 0974, www.jetairways.com, flies daily to **Mumbai**.

Bus ST buses serve most centres of Gujarat. Bharat and Eagle Travels run regular private luxury buses to **Ahmedabad**, **Jamnagar**, **Junagadh**, **Rajkot**, etc.

Train Trains are as follows: **Mumbai** (**Central**): *Saurashtra Exp 19216*, 2000, 23½ hrs, calls at **Rajkot** and **Ahmedabad**.

Jamnagar p115
Air Airport, 10 km west. Indian Airlines, T0288-255 2911, www.indian-airlines.nic.in, to **Mumbai**.

Bus STC bus services to **Rajkot** (frequent), **Ahmedabad**, **Dwarka** and **Porbandar**.

Train Railway station 6 km northwest of town. **Mumbai** (**Central**): *Saurashtra Exp 19216*, 2305, 20¾ hrs; *Saurashtra Mail 19006*, 11535, 17½ hrs; both via **Rajkot**, 1¾-2¼ hrs, **Ahmedabad**, 7¼ hrs, and **Vadodara**, 10-11½ hrs.

Dwarka p116
Bus Bus to **Jamnagar**, **Porbandar** and **Somnath**. Private operators run to most major towns.

Train Trains to **Ahmedabad** and **Vadodara**: *Saurashtra Mail 19006*, 1308, 10 hrs, and **Mumbai** (**Central**): 20 hrs. Also *Okha-Puri Exp*, 0835.

Okha p115
Boats to Beyt Dwarka take 10-15 mins each way. Local buses to **Dwarka**, 1 hr. Buses to all main towns, including a direct morning

service to **Bhuj**. Train to **Ahmedabad**:
Saurashtra Mail 19006, 1230, 10 hrs.

⊕ Directory

Bhavnagar *p102, map p103*
Banks State Bank of Saurashtra,
Darbargadh, changes currency and TCs.
ATMs for foreign cards on Waghiwada Rd.
Useful contacts Forest office, near
Nilambag Palace, T0278-242 8644.

Palitana *p104*
Medical services Mansinhji Govt
Hospital, Main Rd; Shatrunjaya Hospital,
Taleti Rd. **Post** GPO: Main Rd, with Poste
Restante; PO, Bhairavnath Rd.

Junagadh *p106, map p107*
Banks Bank of Baroda, near the town post
office is very efficient and changes TCs;
Bank of Saurashtra, changes currency.
Internet MagicNet, MG Rd.

Sasan Gir National Park *p108*
There's a health centre, post office and bank
at Sasan, and a market at Talala. The post
office in the village has an excellent 'frank'
for postcards/letters.

Diu *p110, maps p110 and p112*
Banks State Bank of Saurashtra, near Fish
Market opposite **Nilesh** hotel, has an ATM.
Authorised foreign exchange dealers next to
Reshma Travels and **Alishan Hotel** are more
efficient for exchange (sterling, euro and US
dollar TCs and currency). **Internet** Deepee
Telecom and Cyber Café, Bunder Chowk.
Medical services Manesh Medical Store
is a pharmacy with a doctor in the building.
Post The main post office is on Bunder
Chowk, the other is at Ghogla.

Porbandar *p114, map p115*
Banks Bank of India, Kedareshwar Rd,
and **State Bank of India**, MG Rd (and sometimes **Bank of Baroda**) change TCs of reputed
companies. After frauds and fake notes, they
are wary of currency.

Jamnagar *p115*
Banks and internet Money exchange and
internet are around Teen Batti in the New Town
Centre. **Post** Head Post Office at Chandni
Chowk. Forestry Office, T0288-255 2077.

Kachchh (Kutch)

*The scenic Maliya Miyana bridge, across salt marshes often filled
with birds, gives a beguilingly attractive impression of the gateway to
Kachchh. Yet this region is climatically perhaps the least appealing of
Gujarat, and it is certainly the most sparsely populated. It is well and
truly off the tourist trail. The various communities such as Rabaris,
Ahirs and Meghwals each have a distinct dress that is still an integral
part of daily life, and each practise a particular craft – a fact that is
being fostered and promoted by a number of co-operatives and
NGOs. For the adventurous traveller willing to forego such luxuries
as hot showers and reliable bus timetables, Kachchh offers some
fascinating opportunities for adventurous, life-affirming travel.*

Background

The central peninsula of Kachchh is surrounded by the seasonally flooded Great and Little
Ranns. The Gulf of Kachchh to the south, a large inlet of the Arabian Sea, has a marine
national park and sanctuary with 42 islands and a whole range of reefs, mudflats, coastal
salt marsh and India's largest area of mangrove swamps. The **Kachchh Peninsula** is
relatively high, covered with sheets of volcanic lava but with often saline soil. When you
drive out to the Great Rann of Kachchh it's like driving to the end of the world. You look
out onto a white horizon and stand on a bed of salt. Dry and rocky, there is little natural
surface water though there are many artificial tanks and reservoirs. Intensive grazing has
inhibited the development of the rich vegetation around the tanks characteristic of
neighbouring Sindh in Pakistan, and there is only sparse woodland along the often dry
river beds. The wetlands are severely over-exploited, but some of the lakes are important
seasonal homes for migratory birds including pelicans and cormorants. The **Rann of
Kachchh** in the north runs imperceptibly into the Thar Desert. A hard smooth bed of dried
mud in the dry season, some vegetation survives, concentrated on little grassy islands
called *bets*, which remain above water level when the monsoons flood the mudflats.

With the arrival of the southwest monsoon in June the saltwater of the Gulf of Kachchh
invades the Rann and the Rajasthan rivers pour fresh water into it. It then becomes an
inland sea and Kachchh virtually becomes an island. From December to February, the
Great Rann is the winter home of migratory **flamingos** when they arrive near **Khavda**.
There are also sand grouse, imperial grouse, pelicans and avocets.

Local traditional **embroidery** and **weaving** is particularly prized. Kachchh is an
extraordinary place for tribal peoples and their crafts. When the monsoons flooded vast
areas of Kachchh, farming had to be abandoned and handicrafts flourished which not
only gave expression to artistic skills but also provided a means of earning a living.
Mirrorwork, Kachchh appliqué and embroidery with beads, *bandhani* (tie-dye),

embroidery on leather, gold and silver jewellery, gilding and enamelling and colourful wool-felt *namda* rugs are available.

Bhuj → *For listings, see pages 137-140. Phone code: 02832. Population: 120,000.*

The devastating earthquake in January 2001, which hit 7.7 on the Richter scale and claimed around 20,000 lives, had its epicentre a few kilometres from this old walled town with its tightly packed maze of narrow winding streets. Much was destroyed, and most of the town's picturesque heritage buildings suffered extensive damage. Some of the structures described below are being restored by experts, but a number of treasures have been lost permanently. Walking through the old palaces like Rao Lakha and the Aina Mahal, where debris of stone pillars and carved wooden screens still lies scattered in piles on the ground, can be a haunting experience. The old part of Bhuj still retains its magic though.

Vast amounts of money and manpower have been poured into Bhuj for the recovery effort, and the rapidly transforming town has gained prosperous-looking new suburbs, a university and a broad-gauge railway line – perhaps at the cost of some of its cultural identity. Nevertheless, it still forms a hub of trade for scores of tribal villages, and visitors can expect a genuine warm welcome from a town still getting back on its feet.

Ins and outs
Getting there Bhuj airport is served by daily Jet Airways flights from Mumbai. Trains from Mumbai and Ahmedabad arrive at the station 2 km north of the centre, with auto-rickshaws for the transfer to town. Buses arrive at the ST stand on the southern edge of the old town. ▸▸ *See Transport, page 139.*

Getting around Most places of interest in town can be easily reached on foot, with auto-rickshaws and local buses on hand for journeys to surrounding towns.

Tourist Information Aina Mahal Trust ① *in Rao Lakha Palace complex, T02832-220004, T(0)9374-235379, Mon-Sat 0900-1200, 1500-1800.* A very helpful Mr Jethi, T02832-220004, sells copies of his comprehensive guide to Kachchh.

Sights
Among the old buildings in the citadel is the palace of **Rao Lakha** (circa 1752), the fortunate patron of Ramsingh Malam, who after his European adventures became a master clockmaker, architect, glass-blower, tile-maker and much more. A large white mansion with carvings and fretwork, the palace contains a Darbar Hall, State Apartments and the noted **Aina Mahal** (Mirror Palace) ① *0900-1200, 1500-1800, closed Sat, Rs 10, camera Rs 30, video Rs 100.* Some items such as glass paintings have been destroyed, but the exquisite ivory inlaid doors (circa 1708), china floor tiles and marble walls covered with mirrors and gilt decorations could be restored.

The **Fuvara Mahal** (Music Room) ① *next door, included with Aina Mahal ticket, same opening times,* is a curiosity. Surrounded by a narrow walkway, the pleasure hall is a shallow tiled pool with a central platform where the Maharao sat in cool comfort to listen to music, watch dancers or recite his poetry. With its entrance shielded from the hot sun, the candlelit interior with embroidered wall hangings provided a welcome refuge.

Ingenious pumps raised water to the tank above to feed the pool with sprinkling fountains. Restoration work is in progress.

Rao Pragmalji's Palace (Prag Mahal) ① *daily 0900-1200, 1500-1800, Rs 10*, built 1865 in red brick, is across the courtyard. The elaborate anachronism was designed by the British engineer Colonel Wilkins (though some guides will say by an Italian architect). It contained a vast Darbar Hall, with verandas, corner towers and zenanas all opulently

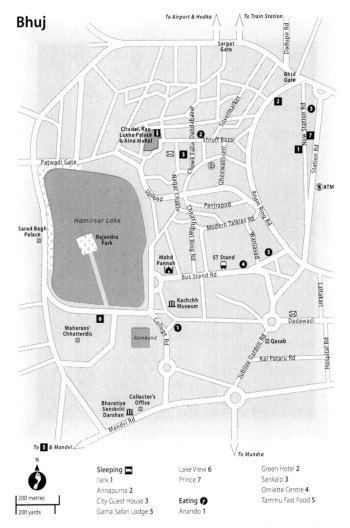

Bhuj

To Airport & Hodka

To Train Station

Dadupir Rd

Sarpat Gate

Bhid Gate

New Station Rd

Citadel, Rao Lakha Palace & Aina Mahal

Chowk Falia Dandabazar

Shroff Bazar

Silvermarket

Station Rd

ATM

Patwadi Gate

Uplipad

Nagar Chakto

Gheewallisett

Chhathari Ring Road

Panjrapod

Anam Ring Rd

Sarad Bagh Palace

Hamirsar Lake

Rajendra Park

Modern Talkies Rd

Wanjavad

Mohd Pannah

ST Stand

Bus Stand Rd

Kachchh Museum

College Rd

Dadawadi

Laltakan

Hospital Rd

Maharaos' Chhatterdis

Ramkund

Jubilee Garden Rd

Qasab

Kai Pataru Rd

Bharatiya Sanskriti Darshan

Collector's Office

Mandvi Rd

To 5 & Mandvi

To Mundra

N

200 metres

200 yards

Sleeping	Lake View 6	Green Hotel 2
Ilark 1	Prince 7	Sankalp 3
Annapurna 2		Omlette Centre 4
City Guest House 3	Eating	Tammu Fast Food 5
Garha Safari Lodge 5	Anando 1	

A melting pot of cultures

Kachchh is a meeting point of Sindhi, Gujarati, Muslim and Rajasthani cultures; the local language is more Sindhi than Gujarati. The arid grasslands to the north, south and west of Bhuj are home to several pastoral tribes: the Bharwad goat herds and shepherds, the Rabari camel and cattle herders, Maldhars who keep buffaloes, Samra and Sindhi Muslim cameleers and others. The communities have Lohan merchants, Langa musicians of the Indian desert and Kanbi Patel agriculturalists among them. They came from near and far; the Sodha Rajputs originated from the area neighbouring Rajasthan now in Pakistan, the Jats from Baluchistan, while the Sindhis claim Abyssinian descent.

decorated with carving, gilding, Minton tiles and marble. The upper floors suffered serious damage in the earthquake. There are good views of the surrounding countryside from the tall clock tower connected to the palace by covered galleries. The colourful **Swaminarayan Temple** is behind the palace near the lake.

The Italianate **Kachchh Museum** (1877), near Mahadev Gate, is the oldest in Gujarat. It exhibits the largest collection of Kshatrap inscriptions (the earliest, dating from AD 89), textiles and an anthropological section. Anyone interested in local traditional folk music and instruments may contact Mr UP Jadia here.

Bharatiya Sanskriti Darshan ① *Mandvi Rd, near Collector's Office, Wed-Mon 1100-1700, Rs 50*, is a small, delightful folk museum and reference library. The collection of 4500 exhibits includes traditional handicrafts, textiles, weaponry and other historic and artistic artefacts, as well as a recreated village of typical Kachchhi *bhungas* (huts) of different communities. *Kutch – People and their handicrafts*, by PJ Jethi (Rs 100), and postcards are for sale.

Sarad Bagh Palace ① *west of Hamirsar, Sat-Thu 0900-1200, 1500-1800, Rs 10, camera Rs 30, video Rs 100*, the last residence of the Maharao (died 1991) is set in lovely gardens. Exhibits include furniture and exotic ornaments. Further south, the Maharaos' *chhatterdis* (memorial tombs), built of red sandstone, were severely damaged in the 1819 earthquake and again in 2001. Some are beyond repair. **Ramkund**, nearby, has a stone-lined tank with carvings of Hindu deities.

Qasab ① *11 Nootan Colony, behind Santoshi Mata Mandir, south of town centre,* is an outlet for **KMVS** (**Kutch Mahila Vikas Sangathan**), a collective of 1200 craftswomen from 130 local villages who are practising and refining their traditional skills to produce high-quality Indian and Western clothes, home furnishings and leather goods. The women market the products themselves, bypassing an intermediary, thus controlling the speed and quality of production and achieving a fairer deal for themselves and their producer group. Their collection and craftsmanship is outstanding. ▸▸ *See Shopping, page 139.*

Around Bhuj

Rudrani Dam ① *14 km north, 30-min drive from Bhuj on the Sumrasar road,* has the colourful **Rudramata Temple**, originally 17th-century, nearby. The goddess Sati's 'rudra' (frightening) aspect is believed to have fallen on this spot and is hence a place of pilgrimage.

Craft villages → *For listings, see pages 137-140. Population: 37,000.*

Handicrafts are a living tradition of Kachchh and the girls of various communities make beautifully embroidered garments for their own trousseaus while women produce attractive fabrics for a second income. Some men, too, are working on handblock prints like the Khatri family in Ajrakhpur. Some visitors to villages near Bhuj are disappointed to find that the previously nomadic tribes are being housed in whitewashed urban housing in expanded older villages that are losing their traditional architecture. Cement and modern materials are replacing mud walls and cow dung. However, the handicrafts of these villages are still of a high standard.

North of Bhuj

① Permits are required for visits to many communities. Apply with passport and visa plus photocopies to the District Superintendent's Office near Kachchh Museum. Closed on Sun. Buses from the ST stand in Bhuj go to the main villages, often just once a day (check time). For more flexibility arrange a taxi or hire a motorbike. There is little official accommodation, but villagers will readily find you a bed somewhere. The visitor book at the Annapurna Hotel (see page 137) is full of practical tips on travel in this region.

The vast grasslands of **Banni** meet the Great Rann in the Khavda region, north of Bhuj. They are home to numerous pastoral nomadic, semi-nomadic and resident people who keep sheep, goats, camels, buffaloes and other livestock. The 40 or so hamlets here are best known for the minute detail of their embroidery. More recently, these villages have started focusing on selling handicrafts as their main source of income and there are signs of modernization and commercialization. The traditional *bhungas* (circular huts with sloping thatched roofs) are made from mud plastered with cow dung which are often decorated with hand-painted floral patterns and inlaid with mirrors during festivals. Traditional utensils are still used for cooking, eating and storage in the houses. The area is known for its raptors – eagles, vultures and other birds of prey.

Dhorodo, 80 km north, is the centre for Mutua embroidery, using chain stitches inset with small mirrors, leather embroidery as well as silver jewellery.

Sumrasar, 25 km northeast, is famous for its Ahir embroidery and Soof embroidery of the Sodhas, done without a plan but by counting the warp and weft of the material. Kala Raksha *① Parkar Vas, Sumrasar Sheikh, near Collector's Office, T02832-277237, www.kala-raksha.org*, is a grassroots organization that maintains a small but fascinating **museum of heirloom textiles** – it's an amazing collection and really interesting to be able to compare the styles of the different tribal embroideries. It works with and trains 180 artisans to create contemporary pieces inspired by their own traditions. It is now run by Judy Frater, the American author of *Threads of Identity*. Tunda Vandh is a good place to see typical *bhungas* of Kachchh. Architecture students come to see, study and photograph the traditional architecture adapted to this hostile climate. The interiors have beautiful Rabari cupboards, chests, inlaid mirrors and paintings.

Loria (**Ludia**), 60 km away, has huts with painted and mirror inlaid walls, and is famed for its wood crafts.

Khavda, Further north than Ludia, in Khavda, you can visit the home of Ibrahim Kaka, where the men make traditional pots and the womenfolk paint them – it is good luck for marriage to have them in your home. There is also a small branch of **KMVS** (**Qasab**) here.

Zura, 30 km, produces embroidered footwear and other leather crafts. Copper bells are also made in this village. **Nirona**, 40 km northwest, has embroidery, lacquered wood crafts, wood carving and is the only home of highly skilful rogan-painting (fabrics painted using iron rods). Buses from Bhuj take about 1½ hours.

Hodka, 63 km north, is the site of an indigenous tourism project, with a resort comprising tents and traditional *bhungas* built in traditional style, owned and run by the village in cooperation with hospitality professionals and KMVS (see page 132). Local guides show visitors around the village, providing ample opportunity to interact with the residents, and to buy embroidery direct from the artisans.

Nakhtarana, northwest in the heart of the craft village belt, produces some tie-dye work. There is a Chinkara Sanctuary at **Narayan Sarovar**, 110 km further west, and **Lakhpat**, close to the Pakistan border, the remains of a port left stranded when the Indus shifted course following the 1890 earthquake.

Charri Dund Lake, a reservoir near Charri village, offers splendid birdwatching opportunities. Flamingos, pelicans, cranes, storks, ducks and other water birds gather in large numbers, especially in winter, while nearby grasslands are filled with passerine and ground dwelling birds. The Banni grasslands are known for their huge eagle and vulture congregations. The **Bombay Natural History Society** ① *www.bnhs.org*, and other organizations monitor bird migrations in the Banni region, and bird-banding camps are set up around Charri Lake. The grasslands are home to wolf, hyena, jackal, Indian and desert foxes and lesser wild cats but are imperilled by the government's decision to convert Banni into pastureland.

Dholavira ① *250 km northeast of Bhuj, daily 0900-1800,* is the site of excavation of a Harappan town (pre-2500 BC), which some estimate to be larger than Moenjodaro in Pakistan. It was only discovered in 1967 and excavation began in 1990. The drive to **Khadir beyt**, an oasis in the Great Rann, through dazzling salt flats is very scenic. Excavations reveal interesting new finds on a regular basis and show the complex to be on three levels (Citadel, Middle and Lower Towns) with pottery, stone cutting, coppersmithing, drainage systems and town planning at an advanced level. The fortifications with walls, bastions and double ramparts reflect danger from invasions or enemies. An inscribed tablet found here bears 10 letters in the Harappan script, claimed to be the oldest signboard in the world. The bus from Bhuj (via Rapar) takes seven hours. Gujarat Tourism's **Toran Bungalow** provides good accommodation.

South of Bhuj
① *Buses to Rajkot or Ahmedabad can drop you off at most of the villages.*

There are a number of interesting villages south of Bhuj en route to Gandhidham, including the craft honeypots of Bhujodi and Mandvi on the coast.

Bhujodi, 10 km southeast, off the main road and a 10-minute walk from the bus stand, is the centre for pitloom weaving. The weavers have now been organized into a co-operative. They produce colourful *galichas* (carpets), *durries* (rugs), *dhablos* (blankets), and other items from wool, camel and goat hair, cotton and even synthetic fibres. Some embroidery and tie-dye can be seen here as well. Mr Vanka Kana Rabari has reasonably priced local embroidery and other items but not the most select quality. **Shrujan** ① *T02832-240272, www.shrujan.org*, run by the astute Daya Nathani, is another pioneer behind the revival in high-quality Kachchhi handicrafts; the shop sells upmarket embroideries and home furnishings. There is also a nice crafts park near Shrujan at Ashapura if you do not have time to travel into the villages north of Bhuj.

Padhdhar, 22 km southeast of Bhujodi, produces Ahir embroidery using round mirrors with floral and geometrical patterns. **Dhaneti** is also a centre for Ahir and Rabari embroidery. Meet Govindbhai, a local entrepreneur, and his friendly family who will show you the embroidered and mirror inlaid fabrics made for their own use. There are some intricate *pallias* (hero stones) by the village lake.

Dhamanka, 50 km east of Bhuj, is famous for its Ajrakh hand-block printed fabrics, using primarily vegetable dyes – you can watch them boiling up natural indigo and making orange colours from old iron horseshoes and pomegranate skin. Used blocks can be bought here as well as an array of garments and bed linen. You can meet Dr Ismail Khatri who is keeping the tradition alive and supplying big stores like **Fab India** and **Anokhi**. He says "True Ajrakh is like stars in the night sky – In Arabic, 'Aj' is the universe and 'Ajrakh' means blue. Clear shining stars show the Ajrakh is good quality." You can also visit Ajrakhpur closer to Bhuj – part of the family relocated here after the earthquake.

Anjar, 22 km southeast, was an early Jadeja Rajput capital of Kachchh, founded 450 years ago. The Jesal-Toral shrine has a romantic tale of the reform of an outlaw prince through the love of a village girl. Anjar is also known for its metalcrafts, especially betel nut crackers and ornaments, *bandhni* and block printing. The 1818 Bungalow of Captain McMurdoch, the first European to settle in Kachchh, now government offices, has some Kamangari paintings on the ground floor.

Mandvi → *For listings, see pages 137-140.*

Mandvi, 54 km southwest of Bhuj, is a pretty little seaside town, with a reservoir in the centre and a river beyond. During the 18th century the town outclassed Bhuj in importance, the sea-faring people dominating the sea trade, taking cotton, rice, spices, etc, to the Persian Gulf, Arabia and Zanzibar. The skill of building *dhows* and boats using simple tools is being revived along the river – worth having a look.

The town is now a centre for handicrafts like *bandhani* tie-dyed fabrics, jewellery and shell toys. It is a desert town but important agricultural research for the Kachchh region is being carried out here in the Gujarat Agricultural University and the Vivekenand Research Institute, to improve farming in the often hostile environment. There is an 18th-century **palace** with an *aina mahal* (mirror hall) and music rooms which have remains of intricate stone carvings of Dutchmen, tigers and dancing girls and woodcarvings in the courtyard. The magnificent 1940s **Vijay Vilas Palace** ① *Rs 5, camera Rs 20, plus vehicle charge,* with huge domes, combines Indian and European styles. You can see the drawing room with royal memorabilia, and the attractive *jali* windows of the *zenana*. The terrace, reached by a spiral staircase, with excellent sea views, especially at sunset, is ideal for a picnic. The beaches on the town side are good for swimming and even camel or horse riding. A wind farm next to the beach is working hard to produce an alternative energy source. The Maharao's pleasant **private beach** ① *Rs 30,* is open to visitors and worthwhile for women to escape hassle from male onlookers. Out of town, you can visit a magnificent new Jain temple.

Bhuvad, Kandla and Gandhidham → *For listings, see pages 137-140.*

On the Mundra Road, 19 km southwest of Anjar, Bhuvad has the ruined 13th-century **Bhuvaneshwar Mahadev Temple**. The *mandapa* (1289-1290) is supported by 34 unusual pillars (square base, octagonal middle and circular upper section). A local legend describes how the headless body of the chieftain Bhuvad, killed in battle in 1320, fought its way to the village. The *District Gazetteer* records that a shrine with a red headless figure is dedicated to him.

Further east along the coast is the port of **Kandla**, built to replace declining Mandvi. After Independence, Kandla was further developed by the Indian government to service the states in northwest India.

Gandhidham, 27 km north of Kandla, was founded by the Maharaos of Kachchh to accommodate refugees from Sindh in Pakistan after Partition in 1947. The enterprising community made a promising start and now the town is a prosperous business centre, though the old handloom and embroidery co-operatives for refugees still exist. The town has developed with the increasing importance of Kandla as a port having lost Karachi sea port to Pakistan. The Institute of Sindhology is researching on various aspects of Sindhi culture.

Little Rann of Kachchh Sanctuary → *For listings, see pages 137-140.*

ⓘ *The southern part of the sanctuary is accessible all year, 0600-1800. Forest Department fees US$5, still camera US$5, at Bajana and Dhrangadhra. Temperature: maximum 42°C, minimum 7°C; Annual rainfall: 1000 mm. Best season to visit is late-Oct to mid-Mar.*

The 4950-sq-km wild ass sanctuary of the Little Rann of Kachchh (created in 1973) and the 7850-sq-km desert wildlife sanctuary of the Great Rann together would comprise the largest contiguous tract of protected wildlife territory in India were it not divided by a road. The Little Rann is mostly a saline wilderness, broken by *beyts* (islands during the monsoon) covered with grass, bushes, acacia and thorn scrub. The area is under severe threat from the salt works, which clear the vegetation, release toxic effluents into the wetlands and pollute the air. A fast-growing thorn scrub – *Prosopis juliflora* – is destroying most other vegetation.

Sights

This is the last home of the **Asiatic wild ass** (locally called *khacchar* or *ghorker*), a handsome pale chestnut brown member of the wild horse family with a dark stripe down the back. Wild asses are usually seen as lone stallions, small groups of mares or harems of a male with mares. Large herds of 40-60 are sometimes seen but they are loosely knit. Males fight viciously, biting and kicking, for their females. Nilgai, antelope and chinkara (Indian gazelle) are also present, but the chinkara numbers have dwindled due to poaching. Blackbucks have become almost extinct in the Little Rann of Kachchh but are seen in villages nearby. Wolf is the primary predator, though not common. You might spot jackal, desert fox, jungle and desert cat on a drive. Birdlife is abundant. Houbara bustard, spotted and common Indian sand grouse, nine species of larks, desert warbler, desert wheatear, Indian and cream coloured courser, grey francolin and five species of quails are spotted at the *beyts*. The salt marshes teem with flamingos, pelicans, storks, ducks, herons and wading birds. Thousands of demoiselle and common eastern cranes spend the winter here. Wear strong footwear when walking in this area as prosopsis thorns can pierce through thin-soled shoes.

Around Little Rann of Kachchh Sanctuary
The 13th-century **Jhinjwada Fort**, on the edge of Little Rann west of Dasada, has majestic gateways. At the southeast corner of the Rann, **Kharaghoda**, southwest of Dasada on the way to Bajana Lake, is particularly interesting. The principal British salt trading post with an old village-pony express, it retains plenty of colonial architecture including Raj bungalows, a cricket pavilion and a bandstand. **Dasada** is a convenient base for visits to the Little Rann. The interesting village has an old fort with wood carvings, 15th-century tombs, potters, a shepherd's colony and nomadic settlements. The Malik Dynasty, who received the 56-km estate in return for military services to the sultan of Ahmedabad, now live in a 1940s mansion, **Fatima Manzil**.

Kachchh (Kutch) listings

For Sleeping and Eating price codes and other relevant information, see pages 14-17.

🛏 Sleeping

Bhuj *p130, map p131*
$$$-$$ Garha Safari Lodge, at Rudrani Dam, T937-433 5853. An option for an out-of-town stay. 14 whitewashed *bhungas* (local-style huts), 7 air-cooled, tribal furniture, hot water, exchange, pool, atmospheric, beautiful views of lake, jeep tours, mixed reports about food, cleanliness and service.
$$$-$$ Hotel Ilark, Station Rd, T02832-258 999, www.hotelilark.com. Hotel with all the mod cons, smart with nice use of traditional textiles. Good food and small branch of **Kala Raksha** in the lobby.
$$-$ Prince, Station Rd, T02832-220370, www.hotelprinceonline.com. Rooms with bath, not spotless but double glazed against traffic noise, restaurant (varied menu), shops (there is a small **Qasab** handicrafts outlet in the lobby), free airport transfer, guided tours of local villages Rs 1500 per car, crowded area, no credit cards, 'spot' liquor permits.
$ Annapurna, Bhid Gate, T02832-220831. Clean rooms but noisy, friendly owners, great Kachchhi cuisine.

$ City Guest House, Langa St, near bazar, T02832-221067. Well run, excellent value, 32 clean, quiet rooms, some with own shower, quiet garden for relaxing, cycle hire, helpful, used by foreign backpackers.
$ Lake View, Rajendra Park, T02832-220 622. Classic faded Indian hotel, grubby but comfortable non-a/c to de luxe a/c rooms with bath, some with fridge, garden restaurant, *thalis* indoors, attractive location facing Hamirsar lake (birds in winter).

Craft villages *p133*
$$$ Infinity, 60 km northwest of Bhuj, T02835-273 433, www.infinityresorts.com. With a nod to conservation, **Infinity** is one of 3 beautiful resorts in India (another is in Corbett National Park). Expect luxury tents and a beautiful swimming pool right in the heart of the Kachcch wildlife.
$$$-$$ Shaam-e-Sarhad, Hodka, 63 km north of Bhuj, T02832-574124, www.hodka.in. Award-winning, genuine village tourism project, very comfortable and unusual accommodation in circular adobe huts or tents, both with attached bath and running water. Beautifully decorated, amazing food and music under

an endless sky – magical. Village visits free of commercial pressure, a chance to contact local culture. Whole-heartedly recommended.

Mandvi *p135*
$$$ The Beach at Mandvi Palace, on private beach of **Vijay Vilas Palace**, T02834-295725, www.mandvibeach.com. A handful of safari-style tents with private bath on an isolated stretch of beach, seafood barbecues on the sand, walks in palace grounds, interesting views of wind farm.

$ Rukmavati Guest House, near Bridge Gate, T02834-223558. Characterful place with clean rooms and kitchen access near the shipbuilding.

Little Rann of Kachchh Sanctuary *p136*
$$ Camp Zainabad, 9 km from Dasada, contact **Desert Coursers** in Ahmedabad, T079-2675 2883. A cluster of 16 self-contained *kooba* huts in a eucalyptus grove, Rs 2000 each includes meals and safaris, recreating a local village, well located, atmospheric but small cots, hard mattresses and sometimes insipid food, a bit shabby around the edges – enthusiastic owner former ruling family of Zainabad, well-organized jeep safaris in the Little Rann, recommended by birders, also camel/horse/village safaris, boating at nearby lake.
$$ Rann Riders, Dasada. Beautiful air-cooled rooms in 22 spacious Kachchhi *bhungas* and Kathiawadi *koobas* (huts) all with unique features amid plantation and farms, tiled hot showers, lovely swimming pool, great atmosphere at night often with live music and tribal dancing, delicious home cooking (especially meat dishes) with home-grown organic vegetables, fresh fish and poultry, enthusiastic owner, good jeeps for tours, whole-heartedly recommended, contact **North West Safaries**, see page 78.
$ Guest Houses, Govt, closer to the Rann at Bajana and Dhrangadhra, where a jeep can be hired for visiting the Little Rann.

🍴 Eating

Bhuj *p130, map p131*
Typical local *dhabelis* (spicy burger of peanuts and potatoes, in a roll), and *bhal* (nuts, gram, vegetables in a spicy sauce), can be sampled on Vaniyawad and Station Rd.
$$ Sankalp, Oasis Hotel, Mews Complex, New Station Rd, behind Hotel Prince. Branch of this South Indian chain serving up mammoth dosas and a mind-boggling array of chutneys.
$$ Toral, Prince Hotel. Good Gujarati food, vegetarian *thalis*; bit more expensive than elsewhere, but in a more comfortable setting.
$ Anando. Excellent for Indian (including Gujarati) snacks. Friendly staff, a/c.
$ Annapurna Guest House (see Sleeping). Very cheap, authentic dishes, homely, allows you to sample each dish.
$ Green Hotel, Shroff Bazar. South Indian vegetarian. Well-prepared food, friendly staff.
$ Noor, behind the bus station. Good, reasonably priced *biryani* and chicken masala.
$ Omlette Centre, near bus station. Popular for breakfast and snacks, excellent filled omelettes, sandwiches and 'English tea'.
$ Tammu Fast Food, between **Abha** (see Sleeping) and **Janataghar**. Good hot samosas, South Indian snacks and *batakawadas*.

Mandvi *p135*
Zorba the Buddha (Rajneesh Hotel), near Azad Chowk. Best-value *thalis* in simple dining area. The bazar has fresh coconuts, biscuits and excellent local corn-on-the-cob. In the evening, handcarts emerge with popular snacks.

🎉 Festivals and events

Bhuj *p130, map p131*
Feb/Mar 4-day **Rann Utsav (Kachchh Festival)** organized by Gujarat Tourism during **Sivaratri** – tribal crafts, folk dances and music, and tours of nearby sights.
Fairs in many villages (*Nag Panchami*).
Aug-Sep Fairs in the Janmashtami area.

○ Shopping

Bhuj p130, map p131
Excellent folk embroidery, leather shoes, appliqué, mirrorwork, block-printed fabrics, painted pottery and local weaving are available. The **market** area stretches from Station Rd to the Darbargadh Palace complex, a maze of alleys specializing in handicrafts. Most shops are closed 1200-1500.
Danda Bazar Al Md Isha for outstanding tie-dye; **Khatri Daod** for block-prints, embroideries.
Kansara Bazar For silver jewellery.
Bandhini Ghar, for tie-dye. **AA Wazir**, opposite General Hospital, near High School, selection of old pieces of embroideries; some for sale.
Shroff Bazar Has craft shops for hassle-free browsing, lots of silver shops, and clothes: **Uday**, T02832-224660, a talented designer (Rs 600 for trousers and top), interesting block prints, excellent tailoring (made-to-measure in a few hours).

A number of NGOs have organized craft co-operatives for the benefit of artisans. **Qasab**, 11 Nootan Colony, T02832-222124 (also has a small shop in **Prince** hotel). Exquisite embroidered goods such as bags, cushion covers, wall hangings, etc, run by informative staff who can explain the process and stories behind the pieces. You can watch as they select and sew. But the real juice of this area is to get out into the villages and visit the craftswomen themselves, for example at Sumrasar or Ludia.

▲ Activities and tours

Bhuj p130, map p131
Arpit Deomurari, deomurari@gmail.com. An enthusiastic and capable young guide for wildlife and birding trips in Kachchh, he has also extended his reach into the rest of Gujarat.
Kutch Ecological Foundation, in the village of Tera, 100 km from Bhuj, kerc@ sancharnet.in. Recommended as a contact

for birdwatching and wildlife trips; they can help put you in touch with Mohammed Daddu, reported to be a passionate and skilled birding guide. Contact in advance.

Little Rann of Kachchh Sanctuary p136
Check with **Rann Riders** (see Sleeping) or **Northwest Safaris** (page 78) for information and guides.

○ Transport

Bhuj p130, map p131
Air Indian Airlines, T02832-222433, www.Indian-airlines.nic.in, and **Jet Airways**, Station Rd, T02832-253671, www.jet airways.com, fly to **Mumbai**. Security is tight. **Sagar Travels**, opposite Prince hotel, T02832-226393, books tickets for flights and trains for a negligible fee.

Bus Frequent service to **Ahmedabad**, (411 km), **Bhjujodi**; **Mandvi** and **Rapar**, **Rajkot** (5 hrs). 1-2 daily to **Bhavnagar**, **Jaisalmer** (8 hrs), **Jamnagar**, **Junagadh**, **Palitana**, **Porbandar**, **Veraval** and **Somnath**. Most long-distance buses are scheduled to arrive at sunrise or sunset, so times change seasonally. 'Luxury buses' with reclining seats, more leg room, comfort stops, etc, are strongly recommended. Many private operators cluster around the bus station, and run to major towns in Gujarat.

Train To **Mumbai**: *Bandra Terminus Exp 19116*, 2030, 17½ hrs; *Kutch Exp 19032*, 2000, 16 hrs. Both via **Ahmedabad**, 7-7½ hrs, and **Vadodara**, 9½-10 hrs. For **Rajasthan**, best to go via Ahmedabad.

Mandvi p135
Bus Express bus from **Bhuj**, 1 hr; others very slow. From bus station, auto-rickshaws, Rs 50 for return trip to palace (bargain). Possible to visit **Mundra**, further along the coast from Mandvi, on same day, and return direct to Bhuj.

Bhuvad, Kandla and Gandhidham *p133*
Bus The bus station is a 3-min walk: turn
right from the railway station. Frequent
buses to **Bhuj**, but very crowded.

Train All trains to and from **Bhuj** stop at
Gandhidham. **Mumbai (Central)**, *Kachchh
Exp 19032*, 2110, 17 hrs via **Ahmedabad** and
Vadodara. Trivandrum: *Nagercoil Exp
16335*, 48 hrs, via **Madgaon** (Goa) (27 hrs)
and **Kochi** (42 hrs). Several local passenger
trains to **Kandla Port**.

Little Rann of Kachchh Sanctuary *p136*
Bus Dhrangadhra is the main transport
base, with ST (Govt) buses from main towns
in Gujarat (frequent from **Ahmedabad**,
93 km, 2½ hrs); some continue to **Zainabad**,
which has local buses to **Dasada**.

Train Trains between Mumbai/Ahmedabad
and Bhuj stop in **Dhrangadhra** and at
Viramgam, 33 km southeast of Dasada,
but at inconvenient hours of the night.
Hotels/resorts can arrange transfer on
prior notice, at extra cost.

❶ Directory

Bhuj *p130, map p131*
Banks State Bank of India, Station Rd
changes Thomas Cook TCs, 1100-1500
weekdays, till 1300 Sat. Bank of Baroda,
almost opposite changes Amex TCs
(photocopy of passport needed). ICICI nearby
has an ATM. **Internet** NDS Cybercafe,
Chhathibari Ring Rd. Good connection, Rs 30
per hr. **Post** Head PO: Lal Takri, Mon-Sat
0700-1300, 1500-1800. Sub-PO in the chowk
at entrance to Aina Mahal. **Useful contacts**
Fire: T02832-221490. **Police**: T02832-220892.
Forestry Office: T02832-250600.

Contents

Footnotes

Index